STOLEN INNOCENCE
A Survivor's Journey to Freedom

Blaque Diamond

Stolen Innocence: A Survivor's Journey to Freedom

Copyright © 2025 Blaque Diamond

All rights reserved. No part of this book may be reproduced, distributed, or transmitted in any form or by any means, including photocopying, recording, or other electronic or mechanical methods, without the prior written permission of the author, except in the case of brief quotations embodied in critical reviews and certain other noncommercial uses permitted by copyright law.

This book is nonfiction. Some names and identifying details have been changed to protect individuals' privacy.

For permissions or inquiries, contact:
diamondintheroughpublications@gmail.com

First Edition
Published by Diamond in the Rough Publications
Printed in the United States of America

ISBN: 978-1-7321141-9-7

About this Book

This powerful memoir tells the inspiring journey of a blind woman who survived years of abuse, homelessness, and betrayal—only to rise stronger than ever. After enduring physical, emotional, and psychological torment at the hands of those she trusted, she found the strength to escape, rebuild her life, and reclaim her power.

Through faith, resilience, and an unbreakable spirit, she transforms herself from a victim to a survivor, proving that no matter how deep the darkness is, there is always a path to freedom, healing, and hope.

This story is about courage, self-discovery, and the power to rewrite your future.

Dedication

This book is dedicated to anyone who is a survivor. Keep breaking free of the chains preventing you from blossoming. Never let your voice be silenced.

Introduction

Hi, my name is Bianca Johnson, and I am a survivor of child abuse, domestic violence, sexual abuse, and incest.

No, I'm not a member of a survivors' support group waiting for you to respond,

"Welcome Bianca!"

I'm introducing myself to you, my reader, and speaking my truth. That first sentence is my truth—the entire truth. It's taken me many years to utter these words, a major accomplishment. I'm sure some of you reading this can relate. The shame and guilt associated with my situation, and similar ones, can drive a person crazy.

It takes courage to admit when something bad has been done to you. It takes determination to stand with your head held high after surviving your abusive situation. It takes growth to speak your truth without shame, and it takes empowerment and inspiration for you to share your story. Are you ready to speak your truth? Are you ready to expose your story to the world? I am!

Speaking up about being a victim of sexual abuse, child abuse, domestic violence, or incest is probably the hardest thing that some of you will ever have to do in your life. Your truth leaves you naked and vulnerable to criticism, judgment, and scrutiny. The embarrassment and shame make you want to run and hide from the world. It makes you doubt yourself and your self-worth. It haunts you when you sleep at night and stares you in the face when you look into the mirror, so you don't look.

After sixteen long years, I finally have the courage, determination, growth, and motivation to tell my story to the world. I'm letting you into my heart and mind. I'm bearing my soul to you. This story will reveal the ugly truth about what was done to me by people who were supposed to love and protect me.

This is my gritty tale of how my innocence was stolen from me. Like a thief in the night, it was snatched without warning. There was nothing to look out for. There were no signs, no cautions about whom to trust. I was blind-sighted, and as a result, I lost the most precious gift that God blessed every girl or woman on this earth to have: my virtue, my precious innocence. The theft of my innocence was a prelude to my endless imprisonment.

I hope that reading my unfiltered truth will give you the strength you need to speak your truth. I pray my story empowers you to come out of hiding. I want you to stop burying your pain deep inside. Stop letting your pain and shame fester inside of you. Let it out! Free your mind from the reoccurring nightmares. Breathe in victim and breathe out victorious! Transform your scars into stars! Stand with your head held high. You are a survivor!!!

CHAPTER 1

At 19 years old, I found myself standing at the edge of adulthood, yet feeling anything but prepared to step into it. My life, up to that point, had been defined by hardship and uncertainty. Having been totally blind since the age of 15 due to years of abuse and neglect at the hands of my biological mother, I was still trying to find my footing in a world that had taken so much from me.

High school had been a patchwork of starts and stops. My mother would pull me out whenever she saw fit, leaving me with gaps in my education and, ultimately, without a diploma. My last full year of school ended my seventh-grade year when I was thirteen years old.

My mother, so-called herself home-schooling my brothers and me since she had a degree in early childhood development, but her version of home-schooling only consisted of us working out of books that she assigned. There was no active teaching or interaction involved in our education. We essentially were teaching ourselves from books. Needless to say, my eighth-grade year was not a successful one.

The instability at home left me emotionally adrift, reeling from the cumulative weight of 19 years of physical, emotional, psychological, and mental abuse at the hands of my mother.

By the time my mother decided she no longer had any more use for me—when I was no longer a source of financial gain in her eyes—she sent me to live with my biological father, Derrick Johnson. A man I knew only by name. He had been absent for most of my childhood, surfacing only briefly and never long enough to leave an impression of who he was as a person and a father.

While I was legally an adult, I didn't feel like one. Mentally, I was still a teenager, lost and unsure of how to navigate a world that often felt impossibly large and overwhelming. Losing my sight had been a devastating blow, and for two years following my blindness, I had done nothing. I didn't attend school, didn't leave the house, and didn't have anyone in my life besides my mother and my sisters. I also had two brothers, but they no longer lived in the household.

My mother and my youngest sister's father used to joke around and call me a white girl. They called me this because although naturally, I was of a caramel complexion, the years of not having any direct contact with the sun caused my skin to lose its pigmentation. Since I was blind, my mother didn't know what to do with me. I sat in the house day in and day out doing nothing but listening to books on tape and watching Soap Operas. My family wasn't supportive of my vision loss, so I had to deal with the deep depression that followed on my own. Instead of showing sympathy, I was ridiculed and made fun of by my own family whenever I would run into an open door or tripped over something on the floor that I didn't know was in front of me. They didn't believe that I couldn't see. They thought I was faking my disability for sympathy, so my mishaps became the reason for daily taunts and cruel jokes.

Due to my mother's on-going neglect, doctors were not able to restore my eyesight. The incident happened in March of 2005, but my mother did not take me to the doctor until October of 2005. By that time, the damage was done. The trauma to my eye had sat untreated for seven long months, so by the time doctors got involved, it was too late. They told her that if she had gotten me help when it first happened, then there was a chance they could've saved my vision. I had two surgeries to see if there was anything that could be done to restore my vision, but the efforts were not successful.

My eye condition and the reason for my blindness is known as Retinal Detachment. The retina is practically the camera of the eye, and once it is damaged if surgery is not performed right away to reattach the retina, blindness is inevitable. Just think of seven months of nothing being done to fix the issue. The human body naturally tries to heal itself when an injury is detected, so scar tissue developed in my eyes as a result of the body's self-healing methods. Retinal detachments occur when there is trauma to the eye such as a fall, punch, head injury, etc. For years, I had been punched in the face, slammed, kicked, stomped on, choked, and beaten with fishing poles, extension cords, plastic bats, cable cords, wooden paddles, or whatever else my mother could get her hands on, so there was plenty of opportunities for trauma to not only my eye, but the rest of my body.

Eventually, my mother found a school for the blind in Spartanburg, SC that became my refuge for the next fourteen months. There I met other young people like me who had varying degrees of blindness. I learned to read and write in braille, and I had O&M (Orientation and Mobility) training, which taught me how to navigate using a white cane. Because I had been out of school for two years, I was seventeen years old when I attended school as a ninth grader. It was a bit embarrassing that I was so much older than the other kids in my class, but I couldn't help that due to my mother's neglect, I was behind. I guess it did help that I was small for my age, and I looked a lot younger than I was, so most students thought I was their age.

The school was set up as a boarding school. I rode the bus on Sundays to the campus, then came home on Fridays. I enjoyed going to school. It was my escape from what I was dealing with at home. I wished that I could stay at the school and never had to go back home, but of course that wasn't to be. I made friends and even got my first job working as a braille tutor and RA (Residential Assistant) to the dorm mother. I learned braille so fast even though I had very minimal experience with it prior to attending school that they hired me to teach other younger kids who were struggling with the skill. I also worked as an RA helping with homework, making sure the kids took baths, and cleaning up their personal areas, among other responsibilities. For once in my life, I felt that I might have a chance to have a better life.

I worked and saved my money in a secret bank account that my mother knew nothing about. My goal was to save as much money as I could in order to be able to afford to rent one of the apartments behind the school where graduates could live once they graduated high school.

The freedom I felt for those fourteen months was short-lived though. Once again, my schooling was interrupted by my mother deciding that she wanted to move again, so school was no longer part of my life plan. My sense of independence was lost as well since I could no longer work at the school.

We moved to Charlotte, NC in 2008 when I was eighteen years old, and I started school again as a ninth grader due to not having enough high school credits and the huge gaps in my education thus far. This school was not a boarding school for blind and visually impaired kids. I attended a public high school that only had a total of about 20 blind and visually impaired kids out of the 900+ students that attended the school. This go-round though, school only lasted 9 months for me before I was once again snatched out.

At 19, I lacked the skills, independence, and confidence that adulthood required. My blindness and the years of instability left me unprepared for the world that awaited me.

CHAPTER 2

The day before Valentine's Day in 2009, my mother sent me away. She handed me $60, packed everything I owned into bags, and put me on an Amtrak train. With no warning or preparation, I found myself on a three-hour journey from Charlotte to Raleigh, North Carolina. That train ride marked the last time I saw my mother.

The decision had come as a complete surprise. I came home from school one day to find my mother waiting for me. Without warning, she announced,

"you're moving to Raleigh with your Daddy."

"What?" I asked in confusion.

"I said you're moving to Raleigh with your damn Daddy."

"Um… Ok."

The look on my face betrayed my shock, but I quickly buried it under a mask of indifference.

"You can look at me like that all you want. Get in that room and pack your stuff."

There was no point in arguing. I knew I didn't have a choice. My mother made the rules, and I had spent my entire life following them. When she told me to go to my room and pack, I obeyed.

In the back of my mind, I clung to a small fantasy. After enduring years of abuse at my mother's hands, I hoped my father would be the better parent. Maybe, just maybe, he could be the father I had dreamed about as a child.

I sat alone on that train, trying to process what was happening. My emotions swirled in a confusing mix—sadness, fear, anger, hurt, anxiety, and a flicker of excitement. I had never truly known my biological father, and now I was on my way to live with him. A part of me clung to the hope that this might be a fresh start, a chance to have the father I had only imagined as a child. I had always wondered about him, picturing a man who might finally give me the love and protection I had never received from my mother.

When the train finally pulled into the station in Raleigh, I expected to see someone waiting for me, but as the minutes turned into hours, it became painfully clear that no one was coming. I sat there, blind and utterly alone, in a city where I knew no one. No family. No friends. Just me, stranded in an unfamiliar place with nowhere to go.

The Amtrak employees were kind. They checked on me periodically, asking if there was someone they could call. But I didn't have anyone. My father was supposed to be here, but he wasn't. After a while, desperation crept in, and I asked an employee to borrow a phone so that I could call my mother. At first, my calls went unanswered, then finally after about ten tries, she picked up the phone.

"H-hello?" I hesitantly asked on the phone.

"Who is this?" my mother asked in an irritated tone.

"Uh… Stephany, it's me, Bianca. Does my dad know I'm coming today? No one is here to meet me, and I've been here for hours."

We were never allowed to call my mother by anything else but her first name. It was as if she wanted to totally disassociate herself from anything remotely related to being maternal. There was no mom, mommy, ma, mother, or anything symbolizing that there was even a hint of care or affection for us. Love did not live in our household growing up. No hugs. No kisses. No affection whatsoever.

"Of course, your Daddy knows you're coming." She replied with an attitude. Let me call Martina, your Daddy's ex-wife to see where he is."

"Ok."

"And here's her phone number. 919-555-1234. Call her to see where your Daddy is, and don't call this number no more." She said, before hanging up the phone on me.

I pulled the phone from my ear and just sat there for a second in utter shock. I couldn't believe that my mother could be so cold and callous. But again, why was I shocked? This was Stephanie, my unloving, cruel, angry at the world mother. Her voice was void of emotion and she was abrupt and short with me as if I was bothering her. I felt a tinge of pain in my chest because no matter how much I wanted my mother's love; it would never be mine to have.

Pushing my feelings aside, I dialed my father's ex-wife's number, hoping for some guidance.

"Hello, may I speak to Martina?" I asked when the phone was answered.

"This is Martina," she replied.

"Hi, Martina. This is Bianca. I am at the Raleigh Amtrac station. My mom said that my dad was supposed to be here to pick me up, but he's not here.

"What in the world? Hold on a minute. Let me see if I can get a hold of him."

She managed to reach my father and connected the three of us on the phone.

"Baby girl? You're here in Raleigh?"

"Yes, Daddy. I am. I've been here for hours."

"Uh… ok. Let me throw on some clothes, and I'll be right there to get you. Give me about twenty minutes."

His reaction at my call stung me deeply. He acted as if he had no idea I was coming to Raleigh today. My heart sank, but at least I had spoken to him.

Within twenty minutes of that call, my father Derrick finally arrived at the station.

When he noticed me, he hugged me tightly, telling me how much he loved and missed me, and how happy he was that I was there. He called me his twin, and I knew he wasn't wrong. My mother had often reminded me, bitterly, how much I resembled him. In that moment, though, it felt good to be seen, to be embraced. It was my first time meeting him properly, and despite the rough start, I felt a small flicker of happiness.

"You are so beautiful, baby girl." My father complimented me.

"Thank you, Daddy," I replied, blushing shyly.

"I just can't believe how grown up and beautiful you are. I'm going to have to beat the boys off you with a stick." He said, laughing.

"No, you won't Daddy," I said, laughing as well.

"I'm serious baby girl. You are so gorgeous."

I let his words sink in, and a warm feeling engulfed me. After years of my mother drilling into my head that I was ugly, unworthy, and unlovable, his compliments felt like a balm to my soul. I started to imagine what my new life could be like. Maybe this was where I was meant to be, with my father, finally receiving the love I had longed for my entire life. For the first time in years, I felt a fragile sense of hope on the horizon.

CHAPTER 3

After we left the train station, my father called a cab to take us and all my belongings to his place. On the way, we stopped to grab something to eat, and for a brief moment, things felt almost normal.

My father and I chatted while we ate our fast food on the way to his home. He told me a lot about himself and his life growing up, and about his family. I learned that my father was forty-six years old. Eleven whole years older than my mother. My mother was only thirty-five, so that meant that my father was twenty-seven years old when I was born, and my mother was only sixteen. That fact didn't sit well with me, but that was the past, so I pushed my personal feelings aside to focus on the present.

I told myself this was just the beginning of a new chapter, a chance to build a relationship with my dad. Although he wasn't around much during my childhood, he was here now, so I would let bygones be bygones and enjoy getting to know and build a relationship with the man known as Derrick Johnson, my father, but as we pulled up to his house, that fragile hope I had begun to feel slowly began to crack.

"Here we are, baby girl." My father announced as the car came to a stop in a gravel driveway. "This is where I live. I rent a room from this nice young couple. It's a really nice room. It's fully furnished with a five-piece bedroom set that includes a queen-sized bed, two nightstands, a chest of drawers, and a dresser. I have my own TV and a mini fridge in my room too."

I was confused, wondering where I was supposed to sleep if he only had one bed.

Blaque Diamond

Before I could make sense of the situation, it became clear that we wouldn't be staying there that night, or any other night. My father was being evicted due to nonpayment of rent. He had come back to the house only to gather his belongings.

I stood there, stunned and confused. I had traveled all this way to start a new life with my father, only to find out that neither of us had a place to live. My thoughts were racing, and my chest felt tight with uncertainty. Where would we go? What would happen to us? I didn't know what to do or even how to process what was unfolding around me.

I could feel a sense of panic slowly creeping into my chest. Questions ping-ponged around in my brain. Did my mother know that my father was homeless? Did she send me here knowing his living situation as another way to dig the knife deeper into my heart? I knew she couldn't and wouldn't ever love me the way a mother loves a child she carried in her body for nine months, then birthed, but this? This had to be the lowest of the low evil and depraved things she could do to me.

"Baby girl, can you help me pack up my stuff?"
"Sure Daddy."
"Grab that black duffel bag off the dresser and put everything into that bag. I'll get the stuff out of the nightstands over here and put them in this other duffel bag."
"Ok, Daddy,"
As it turned out, my father had already made arrangements for us before he arrived at the train station. A woman he was seeing had agreed to let us stay with her until he could find somewhere else for us to live. After finding out this information, I could literally feel the panic and tension leaving my body. I inwardly breathed a sigh of relief. I guess all hope was not lost.

My father called another cab, and we piled into it with his bags and mine, heading to her house. Sitting in that cab, I couldn't shake the feeling of bewilderment. So far, my new life was anything but the fairytale I had imagined.

When we arrived at my father's friend Lisa's house, she greeted us warmly at the door. She was kind, and her friendliness helped ease some of my anxiety about what was happening.

"Hi, Bianca. It's so nice to finally meet you. Your father has talked about you for so long."

"Nice to meet you too," I replied.

"I'll grab the bags out of the car." My father said, heading back outside.

After bringing in our belongings, we all sat in the living room to talk. I shared my life story with them—the struggles I had faced, the abuse I had endured, and how I had ended up on that train to Raleigh that day.

Financial reasons weren't the only motivation behind my mother's decision to send me away. She said that she was tired of me going to school and revealing the truth about what was happening in our household—the abuse, the neglect, and how she had given away all of her other children, keeping only me because she could collect an SSI check for my disability. When that check was about to end, so, too, was her desire to keep me around.

Lisa lived in a small, converted one-bedroom apartment that had once been a basement. It had a tiny kitchen, a bathroom, a living room, and one bedroom. With no other options, my bed became the couch in the living room. While it wasn't ideal, it was better than having no place to sleep at all. For that, I was grateful.

As I settled in, I couldn't help but notice the living conditions. The place wasn't well-kept. Dirty dishes were piled high in the kitchen sink, and the stove was coated with layers of food residue that had boiled over but had never been cleaned. The bathroom was in disarray, and the living room floors and furniture were covered in dog hair from Lisa's two dogs. It was definitely not the ideal living arrangement, but I wasn't in a position to complain. I had nowhere else to go.

I did my best to tidy up, cleaning wherever I could. Cleaning had been ingrained in me since I was four years old as a form of abuse from my mother, so I wanted to make the space as livable as possible. But my efforts felt futile. The damage in the apartment was already done from the years of neglect, and no amount of scrubbing and elbow grease could undo it. The place just needed to be gutted and redone altogether.

It wasn't turning out to be the fairytale fresh start I had imagined. Still, I told myself I could endure it—for now. This was my new life now and I had to make the best of it. I would do what I had to do in order to figure out how to create a better life for myself. I wasn't planning to live with my father and Lisa forever. Especially not in these despicable living conditions. I had to find a way to be the independent adult I was destined to be.

Although I was scared and had no clue how to survive and thrive on my own, I knew that I had to do whatever it took to blossom into the best version of myself. I refused to be a burden to anyone. I would not let my mother's degrading words and comments come to fruition. Because of my blindness, my mother tried to drill in my head that I would never amount to anything and that I would always have to rely on someone else to take care of me. I would not prove her right. I had no idea how I was going to make that happen, but my determination to create a better future for myself than the past I was leaving behind would be the driving motivation for me to succeed.

CHAPTER 4

The longer I was in his presence, my father's behavior toward me became increasingly unsettling. He stared at me in ways that were definitely not appropriate for a father to be looking at his own biological daughter. I knew he was eyeballing me inappropriately because he frequently commented on how pretty I was and even on the size of my breasts and my butt—words no father should say to his daughter.
"Damn girl, you got some big ole juicy titties." "And that ass of yours is fat." "Girl, where you get all of them titties from? You didn't get them from your mama cause her titties were small as fuck." Lisa heard his inappropriate questions and comments and would ask him why he kept focusing on my appearance. Her questions didn't stop him, though, and the comments continued. He even had the nerve to ask her if she was jealous of me because although I was only nineteen, my breasts were bigger than hers and she was forty-six.

Hearing my father's comments and constantly feeling his eyes lingering on me made me uncomfortable, but I didn't know how to express what I was feeling. More than that, I was afraid. I didn't want to make him angry, or risk being sent back to my mother, back to the hell I had been so desperate to escape from. I had come all this way to start over, and I couldn't bear the thought of losing that fragile chance.

I wanted my father and Lisa to like me, to want me there.
I wanted them to care about me enough to let me stay. So, I buried the unease deep inside, forcing myself to smile, to nod,

to keep quiet. At the end of the day, I was still that unloved little girl searching for something I had never experienced. I wanted my father's love. I needed it to be real.

*****

The first time my father raped me was at Lisa's house. I had only been living with them for about three days. I was asleep on the couch late one night, lost in an uneasy rest when I was suddenly awakened by a presence hovering over me. Before I could make sense of what was happening, I felt a rough hand clamp over my mouth, silencing me.

His voice came next—a harsh whisper cutting through the dark:

"If you scream, I'll kill you."

In that split second, everything froze. My body, my thoughts, my world—it all turned to ice as the weight of what was about to happen began to sink in. My brain struggled to catch up, to process the incomprehensible reality before me.

And then, as if a switch had been flipped, my instincts kicked in. I fought with everything I had. I clawed at his face, bit at his hands, and pushed against his weight, but it was no use. My father's strength overpowered me. At only 130 pounds, I was no match for his 220-pound frame or the sheer force of his determination to violate me. He wedged himself between my legs and forced himself inside of me, ignoring my desperate attempts to escape.

He grunted and groaned his pleasure as he had his way with me. Red hot tears silently flowed down my face as he pounded himself inside of me. He talked the entire time while he ravished my body.

"Oh, you feel so good, baby girl. Aah, you so tight."

"I've wanted your pretty ass since I saw you in that train station."

"You're my daughter. You belong to me."

"You know you've been wanting me too, so I don't know why you acting like you don't. Don't fight me. Let me make you feel good. You know you want it."

It felt like he ravished my body for hours as he blamed me for why he was doing what he was doing to me.

"You know you want this dick. Stop acting like you don't. Your mama told me about your little fast ass. Walking around here with your ass and titties poking out like that. You were fine with teasing me, but now you wanna act all innocent. You ain't innocent."

"I'm a man and if you gone flaunt your stuff around me, you better be ready to give it to me." My father wanted me to tell him that I liked what he was doing to me, but when I didn't, he became more violent with his attack. The more I wouldn't comply with his demands, the more enraged and violent he became. I wouldn't give in. I wouldn't allow him to force me into agreeing to his madness. He was a sick individual, and I refused to be an active participant in his insanity.

That night, on a cold February evening in 2009, my innocence was stolen by the man who was supposed to protect me. As Lisa slept peacefully in the next room, completely unaware, I was being violated in the most horrific way. My screams and cries for help went unheard, swallowed by the darkness of that room.

I felt myself slip into a surreal, detached state as if my soul had stepped outside my body to avoid the unbearable pain. It was as if I were standing off to the side, watching this happen to someone else. But it wasn't someone else. It was me.

When my father had finally satiated his appetite, he slipped away like a thief in the night, returning to the bedroom he shared with his girlfriend Lisa. I lay there on that couch, my world shattered beyond recognition. How could the man I had traveled so far to trust, the father I had hoped would protect me, be the one to violate me in the most unimaginable way?

A whirlwind of emotions coursed through me as I lay there, too stunned to move. I felt exposed and dirty. Anger burned through me, but so did fear. I was afraid of him, afraid of what else he might do, and afraid of what my life had now become. My innocence was gone. He had stolen it from me—my choice, my virtue, my ability to decide when and with whom I would share my body.

I was not promiscuous. I was not "fast." I had no intentions of being sexually active anytime soon. From what my father had said, my mother had lied to him. She told him that I was boy-crazy and fast. Why would she do such a thing?

Did she know that he would do this to me? Did she set up this whole thing as a last-ditch effort to punish me?

I had been a virgin up until that moment when my father forcefully entered my body without my permission. I had never held hands with a boy or even kissed one, so to think that I was sexually active was Ludacris. And my father now knew the truth.

Although my body had matured into that of a woman, my mind wasn't there yet. I couldn't fathom how someone who shared my blood, who was supposed to love and protect me, could force me into womanhood without asking if I was ready.

That night was a sleepless one for me. I was terrified to close my eyes, knowing I would replay the horror of what had just happened. I was also afraid he might return; might try to finish what he had started. I felt utterly alone and trapped, a blind girl in a city where I knew no one. Who could I tell? His girlfriend? I had only known her for three days. She had been kind to me, but I didn't know if I could trust her. What if she turned a blind eye to what he had done? What if she was okay with it?

In desperation, I took the hottest shower of my life, scrubbing at my skin until it felt raw. I wanted to rid myself of the filth and shame, to wash away the invisible stains that felt etched into my body. I thought that if I could burn away the surface of my skin, I could cleanse myself of the sin I had been unwillingly forced to commit—the sin of fornication. The sin of incest.

That night, I lost more than my innocence. I lost my sense of self, my trust in the world, and the wide-eyed girl I had been just hours before. When the morning came, I was no longer the same. I felt hollow and numb, as though the person I had been had died on that couch.

My father, however, acted as if nothing had happened. He tried to talk to me, interact with me, and laugh like it was just another day. But I had seen the monster beneath his mask. I could no longer see him as the father I had hoped for; all I saw was the man who had stolen my sense of safety. The monster who had betrayed me in the worst way possible.

Lisa noticed a change in me that next morning. I was no longer talking animatedly like I was only the day before. I toyed with the food on my plate since I had no appetite for food. She kept asking if I was okay. I lied, of course, telling her that I was fine. But deep inside, I wasn't fine. I was dying. I was blind, alone, and trapped with a monster who was supposed to be my father.

I didn't know how I was going to get myself out of this situation. What could I do? Who could I turn to? My mother didn't want me, and my father wanted me, but not in the way a father is supposed to want a daughter. The two people in this world who were supposed to love and protect me turned out to be the ones who would cause me the most pain.

At that moment a realization came to me. I didn't have any parents. I had been born to donors. Sperm and egg donors. The biological ability to produce a child didn't make them a mother or father. They were just fortunate enough to have the right equipment to bring forth life. Me. And that's all they had ever done for me.

CHAPTER 5

That night on the couch was just the beginning. It was the first in what became an ongoing cycle of sexual abuse at the hands of my father. If I had thought the 19 years of pain and suffering inflicted by my mother were hell, I quickly realized I had only traded one form of torment for another. I had left one abusive parent and fallen straight into the clutches of another.

We stayed at Lisa's house for about a week before the two of them had a heated argument. I didn't know the specific details of their fight, but I suspected it had to do with my father's other women. I would hear him sneaking to go outside to whisper on the phone, and I knew he was talking to other women.

Lisa's patience finally wore out, and she told him he had to leave. She offered to let me stay with her, but my father refused, insisting that wherever he went, I would go too. I felt that I didn't have a choice but to go with him.

My father stepped outside to call one of his other lady friends, and she agreed to pay for us to stay in a hotel for two weeks. At first, I thought having privacy might bring some relief from the awkward and uncomfortable situation with my father, but I was wrong. With the seclusion of the hotel, my father's abuse only escalated. He no longer waited until nighttime to have his way with me. He had free rein to do whatever he wanted, whenever he wanted.

When I resisted, when I tried to refuse his advances, he would severely punish me. The beatings became part of my daily life. If I fought back, he would slam me to the ground, stomp on me, choke me, or use his fists to force me into submission. When physical violence wasn't enough, he turned to threats—promising to kill me if I didn't comply. I was a prisoner in that hotel room, held captive not only by his violence but by my blindness.

He took my white cane, my only means of navigating the world, and hid it from me. Without it, I couldn't leave. He ensured I was entirely dependent on him, cutting off any chance of escape.

******

I discovered that my father was addicted to drugs—crack, marijuana, pills, and anything else he could get his hands on. His addiction fueled his rage and deepened my fear. When he was high, it gave him inhuman strength. He would pick me up by my neck and slam me into the wall, or he would throw me across the room with very little effort.

"Do you think I'm playing with you girl?" my father yelled.

"No Daddy, I'm sorry," I cried, feebly trying to pry his hands from around my neck.

"When I say I want some pussy, you give me some pussy. Do you hear me? You belong to me, and I have the right to do what the hell I want to you."

The daily beatings my father inflicted on me never left any visible marks. At least not any that could be seen by others. Clothing hid the bumps, lumps, and bruises that were a result of my father's frequent attacks. My body bore a roadmap of scars that told a horrendous tale.

When the pre-paid two weeks at the hotel ended, my father announced that I needed to find a job to contribute financially to our living arrangements since his friend wasn't paying for the room anymore. He told me his workplace was hiring and took me to apply. To my surprise, I got the job on the spot. No prior job experience was necessary, and I was thankful for that.

For the first time since walking into Lisa's house, I felt a flicker of hope. I thought that earning my own money again would allow me to save for an escape plan. Being around other people, even if just at work, felt like a chance to tell someone what was happening to me.

But my father had thought about that possibility ahead of time, so he was ready. He hovered over me constantly, ensuring I was never alone.

At work, he watched me like a hawk, treating me more like a girlfriend than a daughter. If I went to the bathroom, he waited outside to escort me back to my workstation. If I took a break or ate lunch, I always had to do it with him.

"Derrick, why are you always hovering over that girl? Let her be breathe." A man shouted, laughing.

"You act like she's your girlfriend instead of your daughter," someone else commented.

"Shut the fuck up and mind y'all business. This is my daughter, and I can do what the hell I want." My father always responded.

"It aint natural the way he is treating that girl. He won't let anybody get near her. I know that's his daughter and all, but dang. He needs to ease up." I heard a woman whisper.

I felt trapped, isolated, and helpless. My plans for escape crumbled under his relentless control. My job, which I had hoped would bring freedom, became another prison. My father had taken over every aspect of my life, ensuring there was no way out.

The weight of my father's control and abuse was crushing me. It wasn't just my body that bore the burden of his violence; it was my mind. The stress of everything I was enduring manifested as relentless migraines that plagued me daily, each one more excruciating than the last. I felt like I was crumbling under the pressure, completely defeated and utterly alone.

I found myself questioning my purpose on this earth. What reason could there be for my existence if the two people who were supposed to love me the most, my mother and my father —were the ones who hurt me the most?

My faith wavered, and anger boiled within me, not just at my father but at God. I couldn't fathom why a loving God would allow someone so innocent, so undeserving of such cruelty, to endure this level of pain and trauma. Day by day, I felt myself slipping further into despair.

> I wasn't someone who subscribed to aligning or labeling myself as a particular religion, but I did believe in a higher power. I was a believer in God. Although we didn't attend church that often when I was a child, on the rare occasion when my mother would allow my siblings and I to visit my

Aunt Teresa for the summer, she always made sure we went to church on Sundays.

I knew there had to be a God because that was the only way I could explain how I was still living. With so many attempts to end my life at the hands of my mother, I knew there had to be someone looking down on me and protecting me from death; although he wasn't making the abuse stop. I stood fast on my beliefs, but the more stress and abuse I suffered the more I began doubting that God was the person everyone proclaimed him to be.

But as if the abuse and beatings weren't enough, my father tried to pull me into his world of addiction. He noticed my suffering, the migraines that kept me in visible pain, and offered me what he claimed were painkillers to help. I wanted relief so badly that I accepted them, desperate to ease the constant pounding in my head.

"Here," my father said, handing me two pills.

They were huge pills.

"What's this?" I asked.

"Something to make your headaches go away. Just take it girl and stop asking me questions." He snapped.

"These are too big to be Tylenol or Advil. What kind of pain pills are these?"

"Didn't I say stop questioning me? Just take the damn pills."

"Ok, ok, ok," I replied uncertainly. Something inside of me was sounding like a warning alarm for me not to take the pills, but my father hovering over me, watching me like a hawk was the fuel I needed to go ahead and take the pills. I didn't know what he would do to me if I didn't take them. I didn't want to ignite his rage and find out, so with deep trepidation, I conformed. I got some water from the sink and used it to help me swallow the big pills.

At first, I thought they were helping, but something felt off. My body felt strange, disconnected. Though I had never been high before, I instinctively knew something wasn't right. I felt weightless, my head floating in the clouds while my body sank like lead. I laughed at things that didn't make sense and spoke words I couldn't understand. It was as though my body no longer belonged to me. I had no control.

I begged my father to tell me what he had given me, but he refused. It didn't take long to realize that my vulnerability under the influence was yet another opportunity for him to exploit me. While I lay there, unable to resist, he violated me again and again. My mouth felt dry as cotton, and though I tried to beg him to stop, the words wouldn't come out clearly. That night, he did unspeakable things to me, and I could do nothing to stop him.

From that moment on, I refused to take anything else he offered me. It didn't matter how severe the migraines were, I couldn't trust him. I would rather endure the pain than risk being rendered powerless again. He continued to offer me pills, and when I refused, he began trying to force me to take them.

"You have a headache, right?" he asked.

"Yeah Daddy, but I'm fine. It'll go away on its own."

"Girl, take these damn pills so your headache can go away."

"Seriously Daddy. I'm alright. I don't need to take anything."

"Are you telling me no? Baby girl, you know you don't tell me no about anything."

"No… I… uh… I'm just saying I don't think I need to take anything." I stammered.

I could hear the rage starting to grow in his tone. I needed to de-escalate the situation before it went bad. His relentless insistence on me taking the pills was confirmation enough for me that they weren't really pain pills.

"Don't make me force these damn pills down your fucking throat. Take them right now." He shouted in my face.

To protect myself from whatever he was trying to make me take, I started pretending to swallow them, only to spit them out later when he wasn't watching.

The migraines were unbearable, my pain impossible to hide. But even as I fought to maintain control over my body, he found other ways to dominate me. He drained my bank account, using the money I earned at work to feed his drug habit. Every time I thought I was making progress toward saving for an escape, I would check my balance only to find it empty. I was trapped, my every resource stolen, my every avenue for freedom blocked.

At work, I wore a mask, pretending to be okay while inside I was falling apart. I carried the weight of everything, his abuse, his manipulation, and my own despair—all while trying to hold on to some semblance of hope. But hope was slipping through my fingers, and I couldn't see a way out.

CHAPTER 6

Despite my father's constant watchfulness at work, I began forming connections with my coworkers. It wasn't easy, he kept me under his thumb, always hovering to ensure I couldn't speak freely or step outside his control. But even under his scrutiny, I managed to forge friendships.

I knew I couldn't just blurt out the truth of what I was going through. If I told the wrong person, it could get back to my father, and I couldn't risk what he might do if he found out. I needed to be careful, tactful, and deliberate. I was in a new city, at a new job, and my father had been working there for years. He had relationships and credibility I didn't. I needed allies, but I also needed to be sure I could trust them.

Eventually, I started talking more with a coworker named Jordan. We worked side by side in the manufacturing plant, sewing military clothing and equipment. Jordan was just two years older than me, lived with his mother, and was an only child. He was funny, easy to talk to, and kind. For the first time in what felt like forever, I had someone to talk to outside of my father or the people he approved of.

Our friendship grew naturally over time, and I found myself looking forward to our conversations. I felt comfortable around him, though not comfortable enough to share the dark truths of my life just yet. He became a small reprieve from the isolation and control I faced at home.

Jordan, however, saw me as more than a friend. It didn't take long for him to express his interest in dating me. I was scared. I had never dated before. The idea of opening myself up to someone like that felt impossible, given what my father was putting me through. My trust in men was nonexistent. I couldn't help but assume Jordan's intentions were like my father's, that he only wanted one thing.

One day, Jordan asked me outright why I always changed the subject whenever he brought up the idea of going out. I didn't know how to answer him. How could I explain my distrust, my inexperience, my insecurities?

"My father would never allow me to date you or anyone else," I answered.

"Bianca, no disrespect to your dad or anything, but you're a grown-ass woman. He can't tell you who you can date. You don't need his approval."

"I hear what you're saying, but you don't know my father."

"You're right. I don't know him, but what I do know is the way he treats you is weird. He acts as if he owns you. You're a person, not a possession."

He wasn't wrong, but I wasn't ready to confirm his suspicions. I continued to dodge his invitations, afraid to let him in. Yet, deep inside, I was beginning to like him. He was interesting, kind, and always had something to talk about. We had something in common as well—Jordan, like me, had lost his sight as a teenager. His blindness was caused by a brain tumor, not abuse like mine, but the shared experience made me feel understood in a way I hadn't felt before.

The closer we got, the more I wanted to tell him everything. I knew if I kept refusing to go out with him, he might eventually give up, and I would lose someone who could be good for me. Jordan became my escape. I looked forward to going to work every day, not just for a paycheck but for the moments we shared. He was my spot of sunshine in the middle of the storm that was my life.

******

As if the abuse and control my father inflicted on me weren't enough, a new fear took hold of me—a fear that consumed my thoughts daily: the possibility of becoming pregnant. The horror of it gnawed at me constantly. What if I became pregnant with my father's child? The shame and disgust that thought brought me was unbearable.
It wasn't as though he was using protection when he violated me. The possibility was always there, looming over me like a dark cloud. When I worked up the courage to voice my concern, his response left me feeling cold inside.

"So, Daddy, um… I think we should talk about something." I said timidly.

"Something like what?"

"Well… have you thought of what we would do if I got pregnant?"

A huge lump had lodged itself in my throat as I waited for his response. I felt as if I was going to choke on the lump.
"And so, what? What's the big deal?"
"" What do you mean what's the big deal?" I am your daughter. We share the same bloodline. Do you know what could be the result of us having a baby together?"
"Are you worried about birth defects, or our baby being retarded? That won't matter. It would be our baby, so whatever issues it will have will be just fine."

"Are you crazy or something?" I asked in utter disbelief.

"No, I'm not crazy. So, are you saying you don't want to have my baby?"

"I… Uh…"

"It sounds like it to me," he said, standing directly in my space.

I instinctually tensed up, preparing myself for the blow I knew was about to come. And he didn't disappoint. The slap that he delivered across my face sent me flying to the floor. I immediately grabbed at my face. The slap had my face on fire.

Snatching me up from the floor by my shirt, my father spoke in the most menacing voice I had ever heard.

"I don't give a fuck what you or anybody else think. You will have my baby whether you like it or not. I'm going to pump you full of my cum every chance I get. You will give birth to my baby no matter what may be wrong with it. We will be a family. You, me, and our baby. Do you understand me?"

He began squeezing my neck as he waited for my response. I gave him the answer he wanted to hear.

"Yes Daddy," I choked out.

"Good girl," he replied, shoving me to the floor. "Now get your ass up and go fix me something to eat. I'm hungry." Hearing those words from his mouth was like being hit with a sledgehammer. He wasn't joking—he was deadly serious. He said that if we had a baby together, it would make us a family. A family? The very word, twisted and warped in his logic, felt like a cruel mockery. How could he truly believe that forcing me, his only biological daughter, to bear his child would create anything resembling a family?

The more he spoke, the more the sickness in my stomach grew. He didn't care about anything other than his delusion of building a family through this grotesque and unnatural act. His words froze me to the core. It felt like no heat on earth could melt the icy fear that gripped me.

In my mind, I swore to myself that it would never happen—not in a million years. Over my dead body would I give birth to my father's child! But my refusal to accept his fantasy only fueled his rage. The threats escalated.

He began to paint vivid, horrifying pictures of what he would do if I disobeyed him. He threatened to kill me, cut my body into pieces, stuff me into a suitcase, and dump me in a river. He promised he'd tell anyone who asked that I had moved back to South Carolina to be with my mother. According to him, no one would ever look for me.

He used every tool of manipulation he could think of to keep me under his control. He claimed he had killed two people—and that he would have no problem doing it again. His words were chilling, and I believed him.

The cruelest of his manipulation was the way he played on my deepest insecurities. He reminded me over and over that my mother had given me away because she didn't want me. He drove the knife deeper by saying that no one loved me, no one cared about me, and no one would even notice if I disappeared. And I believed him.

The isolation, the threats, and the unrelenting control crushed any hope I might have had. I felt utterly powerless, trapped in a nightmare from which there seemed to be no escape from.

CHAPTER 7

Although I tried to keep my budding friendship with Jordan a secret from my father, it didn't take long for him to find out. The moment he did, his grip on me tightened even more. He went out of his way to poison my mind with negative thoughts about Jordan, filling my ears with accusations that all Jordan wanted from me was sex and that I shouldn't trust him. Any and everything he could think of to tarnish Jordan's image, he tried.

But it didn't work. I saw through his manipulation. I knew he was trying to keep me trapped as his caged bird, isolated and under his control. He didn't want me to have anyone else in my life. He didn't want me to find an escape from the daily physical, sexual, emotional, mental, and financial abuse he inflicted on me.

My feelings for Jordan were genuine, but he also became a part of my escape plan. I thought that if he liked me enough, we could find a way to be together, away from my father. But the idea of revealing the truth about what was happening terrified me. How would Jordan react if he knew? Would he look at me differently? Would he be disgusted? I knew he suspected something was going on. He had no concrete evidence though, but his questions and observations made it clear that he had his suspicions.

Despite my fears, I began developing a plan to escape. When our workplace started offering computer classes for blind employees, I saw an opportunity. Although I already knew how to use a computer with a screen reader, I signed up for the classes anyway. It was the perfect excuse. My father, who wasn't blind, wouldn't be able to attend, and the classes were held after work hours. This meant he couldn't hang around without a valid reason to be there.

Two days a week, I stayed after work, pretending to take these classes. Instead, I was meeting and spending time with Jordan. He took me to his house to meet his mother, and we would hang out there, listening to music, watching movies, and talking. Sometimes he'd take me on simple dates to have pizza, and other times, we'd play cards with his mom.

For those two days a week, I felt like I had a reprieve from the relentless storm of my father's abuse. With Jordan and his mom, I could let my hair down and feel like a regular teenager, even if just for a few hours.

Our relationship developed quickly, but even as we grew closer, I couldn't bring myself to tell him or his mother the truth about my circumstances. The shame of what was happening to me weighed too heavily, choking any words I might have spoken. And then there was the fear—fear of what my father would do if he found out I had told someone, fear of what Jordan and his mother would think of me. For now, my secret stayed locked inside, a silent burden I carried as I tried to carve out small moments of freedom.

One day, while hanging out at Jordan's house, he brought up the idea of us getting a place together.

"So, Bianca, I've been thinking about something. What do you think about us getting a place together?"

His words caught me completely off guard. I knew we liked each other, but I had no idea he was thinking about taking our friendship—and our budding relationship—to such a serious level.

I didn't know what to say. Inside, I was elated. This could be my escape. I could finally leave my father and his constant abuse. But the reality of my circumstances quickly smothered any flicker of hope. There was no way my father would ever allow me to move in with Jordan or any other man.

"That sounds great Jordan, but I don't think I can do that."

"Why not?" he asked in a disappointed tone.

"I just don't think it's a good idea. We don't really know each other like that to be thinking about living together."

"But we can get to know each other. We've been hanging out twice a week. We're getting to know each other at work. Of course, once we move in together, we'll still have plenty of opportunities to learn more about each other. It's what people do when they like someone, Bianca."

Jordan expressed how much he cared for me and how he wanted us to be independent, and to live our own lives as adults. I agreed with his logic, but the freedom he described felt like an impossible dream for me. Unlike him, I wasn't free to come and go as I pleased. Our stolen moments together could only happen twice a week under the guise of computer classes, and even that fragile freedom wouldn't last forever.

****** One evening, Jordan and I decided to go out for dinner at a popular restaurant. It was a simple date, but it felt special. We sat at a small table for two, holding hands as we waited for our food. Every now and then, Jordan would gently kiss me on the lips, and for the first time, I felt the warmth of being cared for in a normal, healthy way.

When our meal arrived, we talked about our dreams for the future. I told him how much I wanted to get my high school diploma, explaining how I'd never had the chance to finish school because of my mother's choices. He promised to help me in any way he could. For a moment, I allowed myself to believe in the possibility of a future with him—a future away from my father.

But then, out of nowhere, I heard a voice that made my blood run cold. My father's voice. It was unmistakable and getting closer. I froze in fear, my stomach twisting into knots. Jordan, oblivious to the impending disaster, continued talking animatedly and enjoying his meal.

Before I could even think of a plan, my father was at our table. His rage was immediate and explosive.

"What the fuck is going on here?" his voice boomed loudly.

"Uh… Daddy…"

I didn't know what to say. My words and explanations got caught in my throat. There was no way I could explain my way out of this situation. I was caught red-handed.

My father yanked me out of the booth with such force that my back slammed against the seat. He continued yelling at me, his voice echoing throughout the restaurant. I couldn't speak; I was paralyzed by fear.

Jordan jumped up in my defense, but my father ignored him entirely. He grabbed me by the arm and dragged me out of the restaurant, yelling all the way. The humiliation was unbearable. Dozens of eyes followed us, but no one intervened.

My father had been dining with one of his lady friends and spotted us from across the room. He called a cab and spent the ride back to the hotel on the phone with her, apologizing for leaving her behind but explaining that he had to "handle me." I sat in silence, my dread building with every passing second.

When we arrived at the hotel, my feet felt like lead as I exited the cab. My father roughly grabbed me by the arm again, dragging me into the room. I sat on the bed, feeling sick to my stomach.

The rage in his voice was terrifying. He demanded answers, yelling and slapping me across the face when I hesitated. I finally confessed—about Jordan, about skipping the computer classes, about everything. Before I could even finish my explanation, I felt myself flying through the air. My father had grabbed my shirt and slammed me to the floor, knocking the wind out of me.

He climbed on top of me, his hands wrapping around my neck as he choked me. His screams were filled with rage and jealousy, accusing me of disrespecting him by sneaking off to see Jordan. I could hear his lady friend yelling through the phone for him to stop, but he ignored her. Spittle sprayed my face as he yelled and continued to choke me.

I could feel myself slowly losing consciousness and to my surprise, I wanted it. I was tired. I was ready to give up. I didn't want to fight anymore. If he wanted to kill me, so be it. Maybe I would finally be at peace if I was no longer here. I wasn't afraid of dying.

I thought about how much I would miss Jordan, but the weight of what I was dealing with was too much for me to continue carrying around. I wanted to be free from this life. Free from the pain. If it meant death would stop it all, then I was ready to die. I couldn't live like this anymore.

Finally tired of hearing her yelling through the phone, my father hung up and the beating began. He punched, slapped, and kicked me, his fury consuming him. I screamed and cried, but no one heard me. No one came.

The hotel we were staying in was a run-down extended stay that had a reputation for prostitution and drug activity. It was normal to hear screams from women being beaten by their pimps, so my screams sounded no alarms. The environment was a don't ask, don't tell philosophy. Everyone minded their own business. No one called the police around there, so there would be no one to rescue me.

My father beat me until I could barely move, then he climbed on top of me and brutally raped me while I lay helpless on the floor.

"I will fucking kill you before I let anyone else have you. This is my pussy, and if I ever catch you trying to give it to Jordan or any other knuckleheaded nigga out there, I will first kill them, then you will be next. I'm a man. No little boy is going to take what's mine."

His threats were terrifyingly specific, promising unspeakable horrors if I ever tried to leave him.

The brutal attack seemed endless until I finally passed out. When I woke up the next morning, my body felt broken. My throat was raw, my voice was hoarse from screaming and crying all night. Every muscle ached, and my spirit felt crushed. My father lay beside me, his words cold and callous.

"You won't be going to work for a few days until you heal up. You look a mess, and I don't need nobody asking any questions."

I couldn't understand why I had woken up that morning. Why wasn't I dead? Why hadn't he just put me out of my misery? I didn't know how much more of this torture I could take.

And just like that, my fragile connection to Jordan was severed. I never saw or spoke to him at work again. I found out that my father had falsely accused Jordan of harassing me and he had been fired from the job. No one asked me anything. The fact that someone could be fired based on what my father said let me know that he had clout and that I had no leg to stand on. Anyone that I got close to would become a target for my father. His grip on my life was literally squeezing the life out of me.

CHAPTER 8

With every passing day, my hope faded further into the darkness. My father had successfully severed any chance of escape, and I felt myself sinking deeper into depression. The migraines that plagued me daily were relentless, and I lost all interest in eating. Food felt pointless, everything felt pointless.

My father, of course, wouldn't allow me to starve myself to death.

"Eat your food baby girl,"

"I'm not hungry," I replied despondently.

"I don't give a damn what you say, girl. Eat your damn food before I pry your fucking mouth open and make you eat it."

"But…"

"But nothing." He yelled. "This is my last time telling you to eat your fucking food."

I didn't want to eat. I didn't want to live. I prayed he would stop threatening to kill me and just do it. Anything to escape the unending torment of my life.

I was tired. Tired of waking up in the same hell I fell asleep in. Tired of enduring day after day of his control and abuse. Tired of crying myself to sleep every night.

"Get up. I got something for your ass." He said, jumping up from the table. "You don't want to eat your food; I got something for you to eat."

I could hear him unzipping his pants, and I began to panic.

"Ok, Daddy. I'll eat my food." I replied. "Please, Daddy. I'll eat my food."

"Nah, you didn't want to eat when I told you to before, so don't eat it now. Get your ass over here." "Please, Daddy. I'll eat. I promise." "Get your ass over here Bianca." "No Daddy, please. I'll eat." I begged. I didn't want to do what he wanted me to do. I would rather force myself to eat the food than perform oral sex on him.

"I'm not going to tell you again to get your ass over here." He said through gritted teeth.

My heart began pounding so loud and hard in my chest. I knew if I didn't do what he wanted, it would get very bad for me. The thumping of my heart in my ears was so deafening that I couldn't hear anything else.

"Ok Daddy," I said in a defeated tone with hot tears streaming down my face.

"Get your ass over here and get on your damn knees."

I silently obeyed.

"Open your mouth, and if you bite me, I'm going to beat your ass within an inch of your life. Now suck my dick and make it good. And you gonna swallow every drop of my seeds. You better not let any of it spill. You don't wanna eat your food, I bet you gonna swallow my love juice like it's a fresh scrambled egg platter."

He groaned in pleasure as he forcefully held my head in place and pounded himself into my throat. When he was finished, he zipped up his pants and began whistling a happy tune as if he had no care in the world. He saw nothing wrong with what he was doing to me.

"I bet you gonna eat next time, right?" he asked with a chuckle.
With my head hung low in shame and disgust, I answered, "Yes, Daddy,"
"That's daddy's baby girl. As long as you do what I say, life will be good for you. You make me do these things to you. All you have to do is stay in your place and keep me happy. Is that so hard to do?"
"No Daddy,"
"Now go and run yourself a bath. I need some pussy, and I want it to be squeaky clean. And don't take too long. You should only need about fifteen minutes. I'll be out here waiting for you with hard dick in hand. I want you to ride me tonight. Don't make me have to come in there after you."
"Yes, Daddy."

******

The nights offered no reprieve—I couldn't sleep, my mind racing with fear and despair. Bit by bit, I felt myself slipping away, my spirit crushed under the weight of his possessiveness.

To my father, I wasn't his daughter. I wasn't his child. I was something to own, a possession to control and manipulate. He made it clear to everyone that I belonged to him and that he could do whatever he wanted to me. He didn't care how anyone felt about it. His jealousy was consuming, driving him to insanity.

Even when others tried to step in, he refused to let go of his grip on me. His ex-wife Martina, a woman he had divorced years ago, offered to let me move in with her. She wanted to help, to give me a way out, but my father wouldn't hear of it. Despite their divorce, the two of them still kept in contact, maintaining a strange and inexplicable connection.

I remembered living with them briefly when I was about three years old, though my memories of that time were hazy. Through conversations with Martina, I learned why their marriage had ended. He had been physically and sexually abusive to her throughout their relationship.

She had a daughter, Brittany, who wasn't biologically my father's, though he referred to her as his own. When he allowed me to visit Martina and Brittany, it was always under his watchful eye. He never left me alone with them or anyone else again. I liked Martina and Brittany. Brittany was seven years old and full of life, and I treated her like a little sister, even though we weren't related by blood.

Still, I couldn't understand why Martina maintained contact with him after everything he had done to her. It didn't make sense to me, just as I couldn't make sense of why he treated me the way he did. My father had women all over Raleigh—women who seemed willing and eager to be with him. He didn't have to force himself on them. So why me?

Why was he so possessive of me when he had countless others he could be with without violence or coercion? Why was I the one he claimed as his possession, the one he sought to control with such ruthless intensity? The questions haunted me, their answers as incomprehensible as the nightmare I was living.

Ever since I was four years old, I had always had an interest in doing hair. My older cousin Missy, who was nine at the time, taught me how to plait on a Barbie doll. That passion contributed to lots of whippings from my mother whenever I would redo the hairstyle she had done, and I didn't like it. Eventually, it led to her allowing me to do my own hair from the age of ten. I was also responsible for doing my two younger sisters' hair from that point on as well. Once my brothers began growing out their hair, I would corn roll their hair too.

My cousin taught me how to plait, but I taught myself everything else I knew about hair. Corn rolls, mixing and applying relaxers, braiding with extensions, sewing in tracks, and more. My dream was to become a cosmetologist, but when I went blind at fifteen that dream was dashed. Although I couldn't visually see any more, I never lost the skill to do hair. When my father found out that I knew how to braid hair, it became my responsibility to braid and maintain his hair. Even though he was pushing fifty, he still walked around with braids as if he was a teenager. I thought he looked ridiculous and I'm sure other people did as well, but no one couldn't tell him that he wasn't fine. Because his entire head of hair was gray, I was also responsible for dying his hair and beard. Martina and her daughter Brittany were also the recipients of my hairstyling services.

Whenever Martina and Brittany were around, that meant that I had some relief from my father. I took advantage of every opportunity that I could to invite them over. I knew that he wouldn't do anything to me as long as they were around. I also had a deep-seeded fear of my father doing something to

Brittany. She was only seven years old, and I felt that it was my duty to protect her since I had no one to protect me from him. My father had always been in Brittany's life even though he wasn't her biological father, so I didn't know if anything had happened before I came into the picture, but as long as I was there, I would make sure that he was never left alone with her. If he was disgusting enough to rape his own totally blind biological daughter, I couldn't put it past him not to abuse a defenseless child.

The fact that my father started having sex with my mother when she was just fifteen or sixteen and got her pregnant showed just how low he would go. He was a pedophile who preyed on vulnerable women and children. He had to have some deep-rooted insecurities about himself as a man, so he took that out on people he felt were inferior to him. He preyed on who he deemed weak.

Although my faith was shaken by all that had happened to me up to this point, I still prayed every day for God to free me from captivity. My father would laugh and mock me when he saw me on my knees praying. He would say God wasn't listening to me, and that he would not save me because I was exactly where I was supposed to be. I belonged to him and nothing and no one would separate us. Not even God. I didn't believe anything he said because I knew better. This was not where I was supposed to be. I would never believe that this was my fate forever. Some way, somehow, I was going to escape from my father's clutches. I didn't know how or when, but I knew it would happen in due time. I just had to keep praying and keep hope alive.

CHAPTER 9

Just when I thought all hope was lost, when it seemed as though I'd never escape my father's grasp, the opportunity finally came—an unexpected window of freedom opened before me, literally.

A few days earlier, I had given my father money to purchase a few things I needed. Because I was totally blind, I had no concrete way of identifying cash without assistance, and I relied on him to handle the transaction for me.

To my knowledge, I had correctly separated my money into two pockets: $26 in one pocket for a new cane tip and $3 in the other for feminine wipes. But by mistake, I handed him the $26 instead of the $3. Rather than being honest about the mix-up, he pocketed the money and didn't say a word.

When I went to purchase the cane tip, I discovered I only had $3 left. Embarrassed and furious, I confronted my father. Of course, he denied everything. We both knew he had taken the money and used it to buy drugs, but admitting it wasn't something he'd ever do. He dismissed my accusations, brushing off my concerns like they didn't matter.

Although I worked hard for my money, it was never mine to keep. My father took everything I earned, draining every paycheck before I even had a chance to use it. But it didn't stop there, he also controlled my SSI checks.

When I turned 18, my checks should have been transferred into my name, allowing me to manage my own finances. But my mother had already ensured that wouldn't happen. For years, she had lied to the Social Security Administration, convincing them that I wasn't capable of managing money. Because she was my legal guardian, they believed her.

When I turned 19, Social Security finally required a face-to-face interview with me to assess my capability to manage my own finances. That's when my mother made her move. She knew that if I spoke with Social Security, they would discover her lies. She would no longer be able to collect money in my name. Instead of facing that reality, she sent me away—to my father.

As soon as I moved in with him, the payments were transferred over to him. He registered himself as my new payee, ensuring that my checks were directly deposited into his personal bank account. I never saw a dime. My financial future was stolen from me before I ever had a chance to control it.

I never had access to my own bank account. My father kept my debit card, refusing to let me touch it. If I needed money for something, he would withdraw it for me—controlling every dollar as if it belonged to him. He drained my account whenever he saw fit, spending my money on his drug habit and whatever else he wanted. My earnings, my SSI, my independence, it was all in his hands.

The financial control was just another chain keeping me bound to him, another way he ensured I couldn't leave. With no money, no access to my own finances, and no way to prove I could manage money on my own, I was completely at his mercy.

But soon, that control would come to an end.

A few days later while at work, during our break, I tried again to confront him about the money he had stolen from me. I begged him to give me back the money I needed for the cane tip. We were standing just outside the front office, and the conversation quickly turned heated.

"Dady, can you please give me the $26 back that I need for my cane tip? I really need a new tip for my cane."

"I don't have your fucking money. How many times do I have to tell you that? You better stop accusing me of stealing money from you."

"But Daddy you did. Why won't you just admit it?"

"Bianca, you're pushing it. If you don't want me to slap the fuck out of you out here, I suggest you drop the subject."

He kept denying that he hadn't stolen anything from me. He tried to flip the situation around on me as if I had lost the money due to my own carelessness. I knew I hadn't. I knew exactly how much money I had. I had mistakenly given him the wrong denomination out of the wrong pocket. A simple mistake that could easily have been rectified by him returning the money to me was turning into this ugly situation. I told him he was lying, and that he had taken advantage of my inability to see.

"Bitch…" Before my brain could fully process what was happening, I felt his hands shove me with such force that I went flying through the air and crashed through the glass window of the front office. The sound of shattering glass filled the air. I landed hard on the carpeted floor, dazed and shaken, with shards of glass piercing my skin. I heard someone scream, followed by chaos all around me.

"Oh my God!"

"What happened?"

"Oh, my lord, he just pushed that girl through this window."

People rushed to my aid, lifting me from the ground and helping me into an office chair. I heard someone yell to call the police, while others tried to clean up the glass and attend to my cuts. They kept asking me if I was alright and if I needed an ambulance.

Through the commotion, I learned my father had taken off running as soon as he realized what he had done. Someone had chased after him but lost him. When the police arrived, they began asking questions, piecing together what had happened from the witnesses. Paramedics arrived to tend to my minor injuries, and I did my best to explain the argument that had led to the altercation.

Then came the moment of truth.

The officers asked if this was the first time my father had hurt me, and I froze. My mind screamed at me to speak, to tell them everything—to tell them about the months of physical and sexual abuse. But shame held me hostage. The words caught in my throat, strangled by fear and humiliation. I lied. I denied it all.

"Are you sure Ms. Johnson," the kind officer asked, squeezing my hand reassuringly.

"Yes, I'm sure. This was the first time."

"Would you like to go back to the hotel where you guys are staying?"

"No!" I said without hesitation. "I can't go back there. If my father is there, he will surely kill me. No officer, I do not ever want to go back to that hotel."

"Since he did assault you, would you like to press charges?"

"No, I'm ok. I just want to get out of here."

All I wanted was to gather my belongings and find somewhere else to go. I was afraid of my father. There was no way I wanted to be anywhere in his presence. Not only was I shaken and afraid, but I was also embarrassed. I knew this incident would be the talk all over the plant. I didn't want to have to answer uncomfortable questions from nosy co-workers.

A kind coworker named Linda, who worked in the office, offered to help me gather my stuff. She drove me to the hotel, and as we made our way there, I felt a strange mix of emotions. Relief. Fear. Anxiety. Was my father waiting for me? Was he going to drag me from the car as soon as we pulled up? Would this be my last day on earth? These and many questions plagued my mind as we drove closer to the unknown. I tried to calm my racing thoughts by trying to see the bright side of the situation, but the anxious thumping of my heart wouldn't allow me to falsely believe that I was out of danger yet.

When we arrived at the hotel room, we quickly got straight to work. We packed all of my belongings into her car and returned the room key to the front desk. To my shock, the attendant informed me that we were about to be evicted anyway due to non-payment. All this time, I'd been giving my father my share of the room rate, only to discover he hadn't been paying it. The money had likely gone toward his drugs and his women.

From the hotel, Linda drove me to the nearest bank, where I opened a new account that my father would have no access to. When I return to work in a few days, I would have my paychecks direct deposited into my brand-new bank account. For the first time, I felt a small sense of control returning to my life. I could finally breathe a sigh of relief. It was over. I was finally free!

After leaving the bank, we stopped for a bite to eat. With all that had gone on, I hadn't realized how hungry I was. Since I had nowhere to go, Linda took me to a domestic violence shelter, where I could begin to reclaim my life and my independence.

As I stepped out of her car and thanked her for everything, I felt a wave of emotions. I was free. I had no idea my freedom would come this way, but the nightmare I'd been living for the past three months was finally over. This was the start of a new chapter, one where I would be in control of my destiny. I would make decisions for myself. It was time for Bianca to blossom. No more allowing someone to stunt my growth. I knew the road ahead would not be easy, but it was time for me to carve my own path in the world.

CHAPTER 10

After narrowly escaping my father's grasp, I had hoped for relief, for peace. But freedom did not come easily. Because the domestic violence shelter was over capacity, I was transferred to a regular homeless shelter, the Raleigh Rescue Mission. Being the only blind resident made my stay anything but easy. The staff didn't know how to assist me, and there was no one to help me navigate the facility. I had to figure out everything on my own. I had to provide my own food, clothing, and toiletries. Independence was what I wanted, but not like this. I felt like a fish out of water—completely alone again.

The isolation was suffocating. No one in the shelter had ever worked with or even interacted with a blind person before. Instead of offering guidance, they simply ignored me. No one spoke to me, no one helped me. I was left to fend for myself in an unfamiliar place, still reeling from the trauma I had barely escaped.

I wasn't alone in my room, though. I had a roommate—an elderly woman named Geraldine. But she was not a comforting presence. She was bitter, angry at the world, and took her misery out on me. She complained about everything: the music I played, how long I talked on the phone, the time I spent in the shower, and she even complained that my blow dryer was too loud. Nothing was ever right in her world.

Geraldine was sickly and alone. She had four children, but none of them visited. No family members checked on her. I believed that was why she was so angry—because she had no one. Her loneliness had made her resentful, and she wanted everyone around her to feel as miserable as she did.

One night, her bitterness reached a level I never expected. We had another one of our disputes—this time over how long my clothes were taking to dry in the laundry. As if I had any control over it. Fed up with her incessant complaining, I finally asked,

"Why are you so miserable?"

"You are so disrespectful, little girl. You have no respect for your elders. How dare you talk to me like that."

"Ms. Geraldine, you have done nothing but complain since I came here. I'm not doing anything to bother you, but you always feel the need to gripe and complain about everything I do."

"I do not. You do stuff to irritate me on purpose. Y'all kids have no manners."

"I do have manners, Ms. Geraldine. You're just miserable and grumpy, so you want everyone else around you to feel the same, and that's not right."

Then she did the unthinkable. Ms. Geraldine Parker mocked me about what my father had done to me. She blamed me for his sick actions.

"That's why your Daddy raped you. Your behind probably deserved it. You're so rude and disrespectful to people older than you."

She taunted me about the worst, most traumatizing experience of my life, throwing it in my face as if it were a joke.

At first, I thought the shelter staff had told her about my past, violating my privacy. But I soon realized that wasn't the case. She had learned the truth from me—from the nightmares I had every night. I talked in my sleep, reliving the horror every time I closed my eyes. She had heard me, and instead of offering comfort, she used my pain against me.

"Yeah, I be hearing you at night begging for him to stop. And you be crying and everything. I can't get no sleep I here with you making all that noise in here every night. They need to put you in another room, or something cause I aint trying to keep hearing about what your Daddy did to you."

The words hit me like a dagger to the heart. I had spent every night since my escape wrestling with the demons my father had left inside me. I hadn't even had the chance to begin healing, and here was this evil woman, ripping open a wound that had barely begun to close.

I heard the regret in her voice the moment the words left her mouth. She quickly tried to apologize, but it was too late.

The damage was done.

That night, I cried myself to sleep, sinking deeper into the abyss. I couldn't believe someone could be so cruel. What if what had been done to me had happened to her? Or to her daughter? Would she still find it so easy to laugh and poke fun?

I knew sometimes amid anger, people said things they didn't mean, but this was an all-time low blow. I didn't care how mad or annoyed at someone you were, there would never be an appropriate time or place to hurt someone to the core of their being with a still fresh traumatizing experience to be thrown in their face. Her heinous words couldn't and wouldn't be forgiven.

The next morning, I woke up with an unusual calm about me. I felt as if I was in a serene state of mind. I felt at peace. I had decided to put an end to my pain. No longer would I allow someone else to cause me physical, mental, emotional, sexual, or psychological pain. I was going to be in control of my own life from now on.

That morning, Geraldine had a doctor's appointment, and I knew I would have the room to myself for a few hours. I made up my mind—I was not going to work that day.

As soon as I knew the coast was clear, I went to Geraldine's side of the room and began searching through her drawers. My hands trembled as I felt around until I found what I was looking for—her bottle of sleeping pills.

I took them and walked to my dresser, grabbing a plastic cup. In the bathroom, I filled it with water.

Back in my room, I sat on my bed, holding the bottle in my hands.

I couldn't take life anymore.

The pain, the suffering, the loneliness was too much. I was tired.

Without thinking twice about it, I used the cup of water to swallow every single pill.

Once the bottle was empty, I lay back on my bed, tears streaming down my face, and waited to die.

Why should I keep fighting to exist in a world that didn't want me? No one loved me. I was alone.

I could feel my body shutting down. My heartbeat slowed; my breathing became shallow.

As the darkness began to consume me, one final thought crossed my mind before everything faded to black.

My father was right. No one loved me. No one would even care that I was gone. And that fact made my choice that much easier to make.

And then, there was nothing.

CHAPTER 11

I woke up a few hours later to find myself in a hospital bed with medical equipment attached to various parts of my body. Instead of feeling relief that I was still alive, I felt nothing but anger.

Why didn't the pills kill me?

I swallowed the entire bottle. I was sure it would work.

But here I was, still breathing, still existing in this miserable life I wanted so desperately to leave behind. I couldn't even do that right.

A nurse was by my side almost immediately as soon as I had awoken, checking my vitals and making notes on my chart. She tried to talk to me, trying to offer some form of comfort, but I refused to respond. I didn't want to hear whatever sympathy she had to offer. I didn't want anyone asking me why I had tried to kill myself. I just wanted to be left alone.

Even though I ignored her, she kept talking.

"You are so lucky Ms. Johnson. You were found by one of the staff members at the shelter where you are living. They immediately called 9-1-1, and you were rushed here by ambulance. Fortunately, they found you when they did, or you may not have made it."

My stomach had been pumped to remove the pills, which explained the dull ache in my abdomen.

"Whatever you are going through, it will get better sweetie. You are here for a reason. God has plans for you. That's why you survived your suicide attempt."

I didn't respond. I just lay there listening to her go on and on. God had plans for me? What a joke. Allowing someone to constantly go through pain and suffering for so long didn't seem like God had any good plans for me. Where was he when I needed him the most?

"I believe you will do great things despite your current circumstances. Do you pray? Do you believe in God?"

Silence.

"If you are, I want you to pray for healing and guidance. I also want you to pray and ask God to reveal your purpose in this life. He will reveal it to you. You know that, right?"

I just stared blankly. Unresponsive.

She kept talking, trying to engage me, but I wouldn't respond to anything she said. Eventually, she gave up; after saying she would keep me in her prayers and left me alone.

I lay in the bed, silent tears streaming from my closed eyes. I hated my life. I wished the shelter staff had just let me die. What was the point of keeping me alive if all I would do was continue suffering?

Because of my suicide attempt and my refusal to speak, I was placed under a mandatory 72-hour observation hold. The doctors scheduled a meeting with a social worker and a therapist, both of whom wanted me to talk about what had led me to try and take my life.

At first, I refused to speak to them. But I knew the truth—if I didn't give them some kind of answer, they wouldn't release me. And I was ready to leave.

So, I told them what they wanted to hear.

I didn't tell them about my father. I didn't tell them about the abuse, the control, or the trauma. I was too ashamed. Instead, I told them that I had tried to kill myself because I was depressed about being blind.

"Who would want to live life like this?" I asked.

"Like what?" the therapist asked.

"Being totally blind. Who would be happy with walking around in darkness, bumping into stuff all the time, and not being able to do things that people who can see take for granted?"

"Is that how you really feel?"

"How would you feel if you were blind? Would you be happy?" I asked in a rhetorical tone.

"Well, this isn't about me. We're talking about you."

With a sarcastic chuckle, I replied, "See, you can't even answer the question yourself. You know being blind isn't worth living for."

"No Ms. Johnson, that's not what I'm saying. This is about you and how you feel. How I feel or would feel if I were in your situation is irrelevant at this moment."

"I went from being able to see the world around me for fifteen years of my life, to now seeing nothing, so yes I'm depressed."

It wasn't a complete lie—I was depressed about my vision issues—but it wasn't the full truth either. It was enough, though—enough to get them off my back.

After my 72-hour hold, I was discharged back to the shelter.

Thankfully, I was not placed back in the same room as Ms. Geraldine. Instead, I was given a new room with two younger women. The difference was night and day. My new roommates were kind, and I felt more at ease. I also noticed a shift in the way the shelter staff treated me. They were more attentive to my needs, checking in on me more than they had before. I suspected they felt some responsibility for my attempt after hearing my explanation for why I did it.

But even though things improved slightly, I was still drowning in depression.

I stayed at the Raleigh Rescue Mission for about six weeks, but it was never meant to be a long-term solution. When my time was up, I had to leave. And I had nowhere to go.

Even though my life was in chaos, I still had my job at the plant. During the day, I worked. At night, I slept in run-down hotel rooms, on park benches, and inside train and bus stations. I was totally blind and homeless, struggling to survive one day at a time.

I found myself questioning my faith again.

Hadn't I been through enough? Why was God still allowing me to suffer? Why did my pain never seem to end?

When I had enough money, I paid for a hotel room. When I didn't, I had to find public showers to wash myself and laundromats to wash my clothes. The instability was exhausting. Even though I had a job, my paycheck wasn't enough to afford a place of my own.

One of the first things I bought with my earnings was a cell phone. At least now, I had a way to communicate. It was one small piece of stability in an otherwise chaotic life.

During this time, Martina became one of the only people who looked out for me. She let me spend the night at her home whenever she could, especially when it was too cold outside. She wanted to offer me a permanent place to stay, but she was terrified of my father and what he would do if he found out that she was helping me.

Even though she was no longer with him, he still had a hold on her.

I learned a lot about my father through Martina since she still associated with him. After I escaped, he had moved in with another woman. He had been evicted from the hotel, just as I had suspected, and was using someone else to get by.

It made me sick.

All these women are at his disposal. Women he could be with willingly. And yet, he had chosen to destroy me.

I tried not to think about it, but the weight of everything never left me. I was free of him, but I was still lost. I was still alone. And I still didn't know what was next for me.

CHAPTER 12

For the first time in my life, I was no longer just surviving I was living.

After everything I had been through, my blindness and homelessness finally worked in my favor. The Social Security Administration transferred my SSI checks into my name, granting me financial independence. But as soon as I tasted that small victory, it was ripped away from me.

While I had attended the school for the blind between September 2006 and November 2007, my mother had been required to report to Social Security that I was no longer living full-time in her household. But just as she had deceived them about my ability to manage money, she never reported my absence.

Because of her lies, an overpayment had accumulated.
And I was the one left to suffer the consequences.

The money meant to support me was taken away, leaving me once again without financial stability. But before my SSI was revoked, I managed to secure my first apartment.

It wasn't a luxury home. It wasn't grand. But it was mine. A small, furnished studio apartment became my safe haven. For the first time, I had a roof over my head that belonged to me—not my father, not a shelter, not a hotel. My rent was $500 a month, a heavy burden on my minimum-wage job, but I refused to go back to sleeping on benches or bouncing between hotels.

I learned to stretch every penny, scraping together enough to cover rent, electricity, food, and transportation. I had no idea how to cook, so I survived on quick meals—hot pockets, hot dogs, sandwiches, and junk food. It wasn't the healthiest diet, but it kept me going.

Even though life was still a struggle, I finally had something I had never truly had before: freedom.
For six months, my time in Raleigh had been filled with pain, fear, and trauma. I had lost so much, and endured so much. But I refused to be a victim any longer.

I had been my mother's victim.
I had been my father's victim.
But that cycle ended with me.
Now that I had a place to call my own, I started getting out into the community. I made friends, I went out, and I began exploring what life had to offer. I was nineteen years old—I had barely lived. For the first time, I was spreading my wings, learning who I was beyond the trauma that had defined my life.

And in the midst of that transformation, love entered my life.
My brief romance with Jordan had meant the world to me, but at the time, he had been more of an escape than a true relationship. Now, I was free—free to love and be loved without restrictions, without fear, without having to look over my shoulder.
And that's when I met Mario.
Mario was everything I thought a man should be. He was romantic, attentive, intelligent, and handsome. He was six years older than me, and I was drawn to his maturity.

Like Jordan, Mario and I met at work. But unlike Jordan, Mario knew everything I had been through with my father. And he didn't judge me.

He comforted me.

He listened to me.

He vowed to never hurt me the way my father had.

Up to that point, my trust in men was nonexistent. I had believed they were all like my father—controlling, selfish, dangerous. But Mario showed me something different.

He took me out on dates, surprising me with gifts, and helping me with tasks that were difficult because of my blindness. He accepted me as I was, never making me feel like I was a burden.

Though Mario and I had only been dating for two months, we decided to move in together.

He moved into my small studio apartment, and for the first time in my life, I wasn't alone. Life was good. Having him there relieved some of the financial burden, as his income helped pay the bills. The pressure of rent, electricity, and food wasn't solely on my shoulders anymore.

But Mario gave me more than just financial support, he helped me face one of my biggest fears.

For years, I had been terrified of cooking.

It wasn't because I didn't know how—it was because of something that had happened years before when I was still living with my mother.

Ripped out of school again and left alone at seventeen, I had been left with nothing to do and no way to engage with the world outside of our home. One day, she instructed me to clean the kitchen before leaving for work.

We had just moved into a new apartment, and as usual, I followed her instructions. I washed the dishes, wiped down the cabinets, cleaned the countertops, and swept the floor.

When I went to clean the stove, I had no idea that the small act of wiping it down would lead to one of the scariest moments of my life.

The stove was old, with knobs located in the front rather than on top. I cleaned it as usual, then went back to the living room to listen to an audiobook.

But after a while, I noticed something strange.

The apartment started getting hot.

At first, I didn't think much of it. I walked around, checking the air vents, wondering if the thermostat had been accidentally switched to heat.

Nothing seemed out of place.

Finally, I decided to check the stove—and that's when I discovered that the oven was on.

Confused and panicked, I tried to turn it off. But the oven knob was different from the stove knobs. It didn't click when turned, and it rotated in a full 360-degree circle.

Because I was blind, I had no way of knowing which direction turned it on or off.

I twisted it one way and waited.

But when I checked again, the oven was still on.

I turned the knob again and waited longer.

Still, the oven remained hot.

Fear crept up my spine.

What if the house caught on fire?
What if I couldn't get out?

I was completely alone—no one even knew I was there.

No matter how many times I turned the knob, the oven wouldn't shut off.

Terrified, I did the only thing I could think of doing.

I dropped to my knees and prayed.

I begged God to turn off the oven—because I couldn't do it myself.

"Dear heavenly father, I come to you on bended knees asking for your help. I don't know how to turn off the oven. I'm afraid that the house is going to catch on fire and I'm going to die in here. Please God help me. I don't want to die. I don't know what to do. I really need your help. In Jesus name, I pray, amen."

When I finished praying, I got up and went back into the kitchen. I turned the knob one last time and waited.

Finally, when I checked, I could feel the heat fading.

Relief washed over me.

I thanked God for helping me and swore that I would never touch the stove again.

And I didn't.

For years, I avoided cooking, terrified that I would face the same situation again. Even when I moved into my own place, I never touched the stove. I lived off of microwave meals, sandwiches, junk food, anything to keep me from having to cook.

Mario Helped Me Face My Fear

When Mario moved in with me, he noticed right away that I never used the stove.

At first, he didn't ask questions, he simply started cooking for both of us.

But one day, he sat me down and gently asked me why I refused to cook.

I told him the story. I relived every moment of that day in my mother's apartment, every ounce of fear I had felt when I thought I would burn the house down with me in it.

Instead of laughing or brushing it off, Mario listened.

Then, he offered to help.

Slowly, he taught me how to use the stove—safely.

He showed me how to turn the knobs, how to feel for the heat, and how to know for sure that the stove and oven was off.

He guided my hands, helping me cook simple meals at first. He reassured me every step of the way.

And for the first time since that terrifying day, I started to believe that I could do it.

Because of Mario, I overcame my fear of the stove.

I wasn't just learning to cook.

I was learning to trust again.

I knew I was damaged goods, but he didn't care. Mario vowed he would help me through my pain, no matter how long it took. He would replace pain with love. He made me believe in fairytales again.

CHAPTER 13

Why did I believe in fairytales? Why was I foolish enough to believe that I was deserving of love?

I've come to the conclusion that fairytales are for little girls—girls who still have their wide-eyed innocence intact, girls who haven't yet been touched by the ugliness of the world.

But for real women like me—women whom life had tried to break at every turn—fairytales didn't exist.

It was all an illusion.

I had let myself float on a cloud of love and happiness, blinded by the fantasy. And because of that, I failed to see the truth about Mario.

All those words of love and admiration were mirages, skillfully crafted to make me fall for the lie.

It didn't take long after we moved in together for me to see him for who he really was.

The Subtle Red Flags I Ignored

I was so desperate for love—so desperate to be loved—that I ignored the warning signs.

At first, things between Mario and I were perfect. Or at least, that's what I wanted to believe. I loved everything about him—at least, everything he wanted me to love about him.

But at work, I started noticing things. No one talked to Mario. No one associated with him.

Whenever he interacted with someone, it always seemed to be an argument, a dispute, or a conflict. No one at the job liked him.

I overheard whispers about his bad attitude, how he walked around as if he was superior to everyone, and how he spoke to people like they were beneath him, but I didn't see it. He didn't treat me like that, so the person they were describing was foreign to me.

At first, I didn't pay the whispers much attention. I was too infatuated with him, too caught up in the fantasy of the love I thought I had found, but as our relationship progressed, the truth became undeniable.

Mario was controlling. Mario was possessive. Mario was dangerous.

If he saw me talking to another man—even if it was just a simple conversation—he would explode.

"What the fuck is going on here Bianca?" "Huh? Nothing Mario. We were just talking." I answered. "What the hell y'all got to be he heeing and haw hawing about over here?"

"Mario, calm down. You're making a big deal out of nothing. We're just having a conversation."

"It looks like a whole lot more than just talking to me."

Mario never confronted the man he was accusing me of doing something wrong with. He confronted me. He would accuse me of flirting, of being inappropriate, of disrespecting him, but it was all in his head. I wasn't doing anything.

Then, one day, he did the unthinkable. He slapped me because I had questioned something he told me, and he didn't like being challenged.

That slap was the beginning of the downward spiral of our relationship. Of course, he apologized and promised that it would never happen again, but it was a lie. It only got worse from there.

I couldn't believe it. The man I had fallen so deeply in love with, the man who had promised never to hurt me, was doing everything he swore he wouldn't do.

It felt like I was back with my father all over again. He knew everything I had already been through in my past and here he was causing me more pain and heartache.

Were all men evil? Were they all liars? Abusers? Manipulators? Just when I thought life was finally looking up for me, I was reminded just how much things hadn't changed at all. I leaped from the fire to the frying pan directly onto the hot eye of the stove.

Mario constantly demeaned and dismissed my thoughts and opinions as if I was brainless. Anytime I expressed myself, he reminded me of my age.

He told me I was too young to understand anything, that he knew better because he had lived more life than I had.

He used his age as a weapon to make me feel small and insignificant. His words slowly chipped away at my self-worth. His tone made me feel like a child. Mario was becoming my father reincarnated.

The slaps and shoves whenever he felt it was necessary to keep me in line, eventually graduated to punches and chokes. I lived in constant fear of Mario. I felt trapped and helpless. And again, I was a victim.

I couldn't do anything right to please Mario. He complained about everything. The way I dressed, the way I cooked, and the way I washed his clothes. Instead of spreading my wings and blossoming into the independent woman I was striving to be, my identity was slowly being ripped away. I had to wear the clothing that Mario approved of. I had to ask him if I could go out to meet up with friends, and most of the time the answer was no. I went to work and came home. That was my life. The few friends I had managed to make slowly dwindled after their invites to hang out kept being rejected.

Isolation had become my middle name again. All the dates Mario and I had gone on at the beginning of our relationship was no more. I became meek and shy. I hardly spoke anymore unless it was necessary. I felt myself sinking back into the darkness of depression. Mario was methodically smothering the light that shone inside me.

I couldn't believe I was reliving the same physical, emotional, mental, and psychological abuse all over again. I had vowed that I would never be someone's victim, but here I was—enduring the wrath of Mario.

CHAPTER 14

Mario's abuse wasn't just physical, it was also sexual. Even when I didn't want to be intimate with him, he refused to take no for an answer. He drilled in my head that he owned me— that I was his, and whenever he wanted pleasure, it was my responsibility to comply.

No matter how much I resisted, no matter how much I pleaded, he took me anyway. His wants and desires were always more important than my pain.

For several days, I had been experiencing burning and itching in my vagina.

I had no idea what was causing it, but the discomfort was getting worse by the day. Just using the bathroom and wiping myself was causing me excruciating pain. Fear crept into my mind.

What if I had a STI or STD? What if Mario had been unfaithful and had something he passed to me that I would have to live with for the rest of my life?

I had no proof that he had ever cheated, but what else could explain my symptoms? I had never stepped out of our relationship, so I knew I wasn't the cause of whatever was going on with me.

I brought up my concerns to him, hoping for some level of reassurance or even just basic concern, but Mario didn't care. He dismissed my pain and still expected me to be intimate with him—despite how much I was suffering.

I needed answers, so I made a doctor's appointment to get myself checked out. I asked Mario to go with me for support, but he refused. The man I loved wouldn't even go with me to the doctor—Yet he still expected me to sleep with him? And yes, dumbly, despite all that Mario was putting me through, I still loved him. He was all I had. Up to this point in my life, pain was love, so in my mind, I was right to still love him.

I went to the doctor alone. The feeling of shame and uncertainty made me squirm in anxious anticipation until my name was called. I was escorted back to an examination room after my vitals were taken to wait for the doctor to see me. I didn't have to wait long.

"Hi, Bianca. I am Dr. Pearson. What brings you in today?"

"So… uh… I've been itching and burning in my vagina," I nervously answered.

"Ahh, and when did this start?"

"A few days ago."

"Have you used any skin care products lately that you don't normally use?"

"Well… I just bought some new bubble baths from Bath & Body Works that I used. That's it."

"Did you notice an odor or discharge?"

"I'm not sure about the discharge. I don't think so. But I haven't noticed any unusual smells."

"Ok. So, I'm going to give you a Pelvic exam to see if I can tell what's going on with you."

and after the examination, the mystery was solved. I had a yeast infection. The bubble bath I had taken a few days before had caused the infection. It was such a sigh of relief that it wasn't anything more serious. The doctor prescribed antibiotics and told me it would clear up in about ten days.

She also gave me one crucial piece of advice—I needed to abstain from sex until the infection was gone. Otherwise, it could come back. I heard what she said, but she didn't have a boyfriend like Mario. He wasn't going to go for no sex for ten days.

Sitting in the back of a cab on my way home, I replayed the doctor's words over and over. A yeast infection.
At nineteen years old, I had never even heard of such a thing. And that was all my mother's doing. She never taught me about women's health—about infections, symptoms, or even how to recognize when something was wrong. I knew about menstrual cycles. I knew about how babies were made. And that was it.
Sex was a forbidden topic in our home. We weren't even allowed to say the word sex in general conversation without it ending in a beating.

Once I was telling my brothers about a girl in my sixth-grade class who was pregnant because she had been raped, and my mother overheard the conversation. I hadn't said the word rape. I just said the girl had been abused by an older boy, and I got the mess beat out of me that day. The punishment was uncalled for. I don't know if my mother was so anti-sex because of the fact that she was out there having sex at a young age and had five kids by five different men to show for it or what, but her behavior was ridiculous.

At twelve years old, my mother sat my brothers and I down and handed us a book full of graphic STD and STI images. She flipped through the pages, showing us what our genitals would look like if we ever caught one of those disease That was her version of "The Birds and the Bees." That was our sexual education lesson. Seeing those disgusting images had done its job. I had no problems keeping my legs closed.

Until my father entered my life and my body without my permission.

When I got home, I told Mario what the doctor said. I explained that I needed to heal and that I had been instructed to abstain from sex until the infection cleared. I was better off telling him I was going to climb Mount Everest. He dismissed my words like they were nothing. The doctor's warning meant nothing to him. My pain meant nothing to him. He still expected me to be available for him —and when I refused, he took what he wanted anyway.

I was left feeling helpless. Disgusted. Violated. It didn't matter what I said. It didn't matter how I felt. Mario wouldn't be denied.

CHAPTER 15

Mario's anger issues weren't just affecting our home life, they started to spill over into the workplace as well. His constant altercations with coworkers, his inability to control his temper, and his refusal to listen to authority finally caught up with him. Mario got fired. I should have seen it coming. Everyone at work saw it coming. And now, I was the one left to suffer the consequences.

With no job, Mario had no income—which meant I was now financially responsible for supporting the entire household on my own. But that wasn't even the worst part. Now that Mario had lost his job, his rage grew even worse.

I became more of a punching bag—his daily stress reliever. Whenever he was frustrated, angry, or needed to feel power, he took it out on me. I walked on eggshells, trying to avoid doing or saying the wrong thing, but it didn't matter. He always found something wrong with me.

No matter how hard I tried, nothing was ever enough. The financial stress and Mario's uncontrollable rage were destroying me. The migraines I had suffered while living with my father returned, pounding in my head day after day.

The stress of my life was pulling me into a deep dark hole of depression—The same black hole I had barely escaped before. I wasn't living anymore. I was just existing; moving through life on autopilot, completely numb. Nothing had meaning to me anymore. Days blended together, and I felt nothing.

Our first anniversary came and went. There was nothing to celebrate. Love no longer lived in our home. I was just there. Too scared to leave. I endured everything Mario did to me because I was hopeless. I couldn't help myself anymore. I was defeated. Trapped in His Control

Four months after Mario lost his job at the manufacturing plant, he finally found a new one, but it required us to move to another city. Greensboro, NC. I didn't want to leave. I had built a sense of familiarity in Raleigh. I didn't want to start over in another unknown place, in another unknown city where I knew no one but my abuser.

But Mario didn't care how I felt. His needs were prioritized over mine. He beat me, badgered me, and guilted me into moving with him. I gave up my life. I gave up my job. I gave up my sense of belonging. I followed him kicking and screaming into the unknown.

And if I thought things in Raleigh were bad, once we moved to Greensboro, things got worse.

Now that I was unemployed, Mario ruled over me completely. With no job, I had no income—which meant I had no power. He was the sole provider, and he never let me forget it.

To earn my keep, Mario forced me to work with him at his new job—a cafeteria where he was a manager. I had no choice. Even though I wasn't an employee, I was expected to work like one. I had to prepare food, clean the bathrooms, and wipe down the tables every single day. I was there with him all day, every day— As if I belonged to him.

I applied for jobs as soon as we moved, but I hadn't heard anything back yet for the jobs I had applied for. Finding employment as a blind person was next to impossible due to society's assumptions about what a person who was blind was capable of doing.

Mario reminded me constantly that he was the one paying the bills. He was the one providing everything. He made sure I knew I was nothing without him. If I needed toilet paper, I had to ask him. If I needed feminine products, I had to go to him. He had no problem wielding his power over me in my most vulnerable state.

One day, during one of our many arguments, Mario snapped. We were in the kitchen when he suddenly shoved me against the wall.

"Bitch, what have I told your ass about saying I said something that I didn't say?"

His hands wrapped tightly around my throat. I tried screaming, but his grip prevented the sound from escaping. All that came from me was a strangled gurgle.

"You think I'm playing with you. Don't you? Your young ass gonna learn one of these days that I aint to be fucked with. You must like me putting my foot up your ass. You keep pushing me."

The force of Mario's push caused the heel of my foot to slam through the wall—Leaving a hole the size of an orange. I clawed at his face and neck, desperate to make him let me go.

Finally, he released me, but my leaving a nice-sized scratch across his face only made him angrier. He grabbed me again— this time, shoving me toward the door.

"Bitch, you scratched my face?"

"I'm sorry Mario. I didn't mean to. I was trying to get you off of me."

"Nah, I'm not trying to hear that shit. I can't believe your ass scratched me in my face."

"I'm sorry. Please don't do this."

"Your ass should've thought about that before you scratched my face."

I dropped to the floor, trying to anchor myself—but he wasn't done. Mario yanked me up by my hair, dragging me toward the front door of the apartment.

"Get your ass out. Go find somewhere else to live."

"Mario, please. Don't do this. You can't put me out." I cried.

"Like hell, I can't. I pay the fucking bills here, not you. My name on everything in here, so if I tell your ass to get the fuck out, then you get the fuck out."

"Mario, please don't do this to me. You know I don't have anywhere else to go."

"Your ungrateful ass should've thought about that before you bit the hand that literally feeds you."

"I know Mario. I'm so sorry. I won't do it again.".

While I was on the floor begging and groveling, Mario gathered items that belonged to me and threw them outside. Making it clear that he could kick me out whenever he wanted to. And unfortunately, he could. Everything was in his name. I had no job. I had no income. I had no power.

I continued to beg and plead with him not to throw me out. I had nowhere to go. I didn't know anyone in this city. I had nothing. I was desperate. I said and did anything I could to convince him to let me stay. I couldn't allow him to throw me onto the streets with no one and nothing.

Mario had made sure I was completely dependent on him. And he was using that power to break me.

CHAPTER 16

Thankfully, my bout with unemployment didn't last long—but those three months felt like an eternity. I finally secured a job at a company that hired blind and visually impaired employees to pick, pack, and ship orders for the military.

With that job came something I hadn't felt in a long time— Independence. I had my own money again. I was no longer financially dependent on Mario. And with my pay increase, I knew what I had to do—Start saving for my escape. Even though I had new coworkers in a new environment, my personality hadn't changed. I was still shy, quiet, and reserved—only speaking when absolutely necessary. But there was one bright spot in my new job—I made a friend. Her name was Veronica, and she was older than me, so I saw her as an older sister figure. Our bond was instant, and for the first time in a long time, I had someone I could turn to. But still, I kept my mouth shut about Mario's abuse.

I wanted to tell her. I wanted to let someone in, but I couldn't.
As always, Mario's temper got the best of him. Just like at his last job, he couldn't control himself. His behavior got him fired —again, but this time, I wasn't financially reliant on him. This time, I had my own money.

While Mario was struggling to find another job, my hard work was paying off. I was promoted to a computer operator position within the company. With that came:
A pay increase My own office A
confidential federal security clearance

Stolen Innocence

For the first time, I was truly moving up in the world. I could see a future beyond just surviving, but Mario didn't see it that way. His insecurities began to surface.

Our arguments shifted from his usual control and jealousy to something new—The fact that I made more money than he did. That infuriated him. Instead of being proud of me, instead of celebrating my success, Mario resented it.

He convinced himself that I thought I was better than him now that I was the "breadwinner."

"Oh, so you think you're better than me now since you got that little job, huh?"

"Mario, what are you talking about? Nobody said anything about me being better than you."

"Yeah, you think you all that now. Prancing around in your little slacks and blouses like you the shit. You still aint shit. No matter how much money you make, that fact aint gonna change."

"Mario, you should be proud of me. You know how hard it is for someone like me to even find a job, but instead you're trying to demean my accomplishment."

I couldn't believe that he was acting like that. When he was on top, he couldn't wait to gloat and rub it in my face, but now that the phoenix was rising, he couldn't handle it. I hadn't done anything to make him believe what he thought. That was just his own insecurity talking and creating things in his mind.

I was the same person I had always been, but to Mario, my financial freedom meant that I no longer needed him, and that thought terrified him.

With my increased income, I finally got the courage to tell Mario that I wanted to leave. I told him I had enough of his control and abuse. I told him we should go our separate ways. I was finally ready to be rid of this nightmare that had been my life for the past four years. The biggest mistake I had made in my life was believing that Mario would do right by me. I believed the cotton candy rainbows he fed me, but now it was time for me to move forward with my life.

"I've had enough of this."

"you've had enough of what?"

"This relationship. This life. I can't do this anymore."

"Yeah, just what I thought. Since you got that new little job of yours, now you think you can just up and leave me."

"Mario, you know I haven't been happy with you for a while. And the way you treat me tells me that you're not happy either, so why continue to be in an unhappy situation?"

"So you saying you're not happy with me?"

"Mario, let's not play childish games. You know I'm not happy."

I started looking for my own place to rent. I would browse websites, looking for the perfect apartment for just me. I was already thinking of how I would decorate my place and what furniture I would buy. The thought of finally leaving Mario kept a smile on my face and a pep in my step. I knew hope was on the horizon.

At first, Mario acted as if he was okay with us separating. He even made it seem like he would let me go. He pleaded with me to give him another chance, claiming that I hadn't given him a chance to change. But then—he flipped the script once he saw his begging and pleading wasn't working.

"Bitch, if you ever try to leave me, I will kill your ass dead. I would rather see you dead than let you walk out of my life."

"But Mario,"

"Don't but Mario me. I made you, and I'll be damned if I let the next man get what I molded. When I met you, you were nothing. I made you what you are today, and you talking about leaving me? The only way that's gonna happen is in a pine box. Fuck with me if you wanna."

And I knew he meant every word. He would never let me leave him. In his warped mind, he owned me. I was a possession, not a person. Sounds familiar?

Once Mario knew I wanted to leave, my life became a prison—More than it had ever been before. He watched me like a hawk. He checked my phone to see who I was talking to. Mario even checked my web browser history to see if I had searched for anything about leaving him. He monitored my every move, waiting for me to step out of line. And the beatings and psychological abuse worsened.

"You will never amount to anything. You need me. You wouldn't be able to make it out there without me. Who's going to want your ass? You're blind. Nobody wants a blind woman."

"Then why won't you just let me go if I'm so horrible and unwanted?" I asked.

"Because you belong to and with me. I am your man, and I make the rules around here. And I'm telling you that your ass aint going anywhere, so you can get that thought out of your head."

Mario used every cruel word he could think of to tear me down mentally. He wanted me to believe that I was nothing without him. That I would never escape him.

****** I knew I had reached my breaking point when I started contemplating murder. The thoughts crept in slowly at first, but then, they became more frequent. And then, they became daily.

I couldn't take it anymore. Mario's abuse, his control, and his dominance was driving me insane. I couldn't eat. I couldn't sleep. All I could think about was how to get rid of him.

And the only option that seemed possible? Killing him.

A Dangerous Thought: "Him or Me"

Mario had severe food allergies to Shellfish, tree nuts, and sesame seeds. On his orders, I was the one who cooked his meals. The thought lingered in my mind. I could easily grind up some nuts or seeds, lace his food with it, and he'd never suspect a thing.

He would eat it. He would have an allergic reaction, and I would do nothing to help him. Conveniently his epi pen would disappear, and he would die. I would play the poor blind woman role, turning on the waterworks to explain how I accidentally put the wrong ingredients in his meal due to my inability to see, and I would get away with it.

My thoughts were so dangerous they even scared me, but they felt necessary because Mario had made one thing crystal clear— He would never let me leave him willingly, so what other choice did I have?

It was him or me, and I would rather it be him than me. I knew I had tried to commit suicide in the past because of what my father was doing to me, but I now wanted to live. I didn't want anyone pushing me to the point that I was ready to check out on life. I had so much of life to live. There was still so much I had yet to accomplish. Getting rid of Mario was my only option if I wanted to start living life on my own terms.

But then, something inside me snapped back to reality. I didn't want to be that person.

I didn't want to end up in prison because of him. I knew if I followed through with what I was thinking, I'd end up on an episode of Snapped. That's when I finally did what I should have done years ago. I asked for help.

I had been struggling at work, and people were starting to notice. I had uncontrollable crying episodes due to the stress. I was always jumpy and nervous.

I felt like I was falling apart in front of everyone.

One day, Veronica, my closest friend at work, came into my office to find out what was going on with me, and I finally spilled my guts.

"Veronica, I've been being physically and sexually abused by Mario basically since the beginning of our relationship. I can't take any more of this. I'm contemplating killing him just so that I can be free of him, and that scares me."

"What?" Veronica gasped in shock. "Are you serious girl?"

"As a heart attack. I'm done. I've had all I can take of him. I just want to get out, but I don't know how."

"Friend, I'm so sorry to hear that you've been going through all of this. I suspected something was up with y'all, but I couldn't quite put my finger on it."

"Yeah, I've been hiding everything from everyone. I've been so ashamed of what I've been dealing with, and I feared judgment from people on the outside looking in. People as say you need to leave an abusive situation, but it's not as easy as people make it out to be."

"You're right about that. I've been exactly where you are."

We cried together as I poured my soul out to her.

"I need help Veronica. I'm finally reaching out for help because I'm losing it."

"I'm here for you girl. What do you need me to do? Do you want me to get my husband and some of his cousins to give Mario a taste of his own medicine?"

"Although I would love to see Mario get his ass beat for once, he's not worth it. I don't want anyone getting into trouble on his account."

"Just let me know what you want to do. Are you sure you're ready to leave?"

"Yes," I said with confidence.

"You know sometimes in situations like yours, women get help, then they end up going right back to the bastard that's hurting them. So, are you sure this is what you want?"

"I am absolutely sure. There is no going back for me. I tried leaving once before, and Mario made it perfectly clear that he would not allow me to leave him without me ending up dead."

"Ok, so let's come up with a plan to get you out of that hell hole without him knowing," Veronica said in a conspiratorial tone.

We set our plan in motion. We rented a U-Haul truck in advance, then I arranged time off from work with my boss. Out of the days I had requested off, we decided on a day to execute my escape.

The plan was simple but effective. I would wake up like normal and get ready for work. Since Mario had to commute to Winston-Salem, he always left before I did. That was my window of opportunity. I knew his schedule like the back of my hand, so I knew when he would be home.

Days leading up to my escape, I started packing little by little, hiding my belongings in the spare bedroom closet so he wouldn't notice. Then, on the morning of the great escape, I put the plan into action. I was full of nervous excitement at what was about to go down.

The moment Mario left for work; I moved fast. I packed up everything else I was taking. Veronica's husband arrived an hour after Mario had left with the U-Haul truck, and We loaded up all my belongings. The act took less than two hours. We all moved with haste and purpose. We were on a mission.

The only thing I left behind in the apartment was the bedroom set. He could have it. I didn't want anything that reminded me of what he had done to me. I also left the "I'm sorry gifts" Mario would buy me to try to pacify me after one of his beatings. They were expensive gifts such as Coach and Gucci purses, expensive sunglasses, jewelry, and other blood bargains. That's what I called them. Veronica thought I should take them with me, but I wanted no parts of those items. I also left anything that belonged to Mario.

Everything else? I took it. The dining room set. Mine. The washer and dryer? Mine. The gym equipment? Mine. The living room furniture? Mine. Everything I had paid for, I took. Since Mario liked to use my credit to buy things since his credit was shot, these items belonged to me.

I left one last thing for him—a letter. I typed it out, taped it to his office door, and walked away. Never looking back. Walking out that front door to freedom was the best feeling in the world. I had finally done it. I had finally left Mario.

I knew there was no way I could have told him I was leaving—Not after what happened the first time I tried to leave. This time, I had to move in silence. Veronica and I plotted and planned every detail.

But that last week leading up to my escape?
It was the most nerve-wracking week of my life.
I was terrified that Mario would find out. I had nightmares that he would catch me leaving and kill me, but luck was on my side. He had no idea what was happening right under his nose.

And by the time he figured it out, it was too late. I was gone. I was free. For the first time in five years, I was breathing in the taste of freedom. I was twenty-four years old, and I was finally free to live my life on my own terms.

CHAPTER 17

After leaving Mario, I moved in with Veronica and her husband.

They had just purchased a brand-new home, and they welcomed me with open arms. I used their two-car garage as storage for my belongings until I could figure out what to do with them.

I was free, but the scars of Mario's abuse didn't fade overnight. Even though I was no longer under his roof, the effects of his abuse didn't just disappear. I still had nightmares.

I dreamed of him finding me, dragging me back, imprisoning me all over again. And while the physical abuse had ended, the mental and emotional torment continued.

Mario harassed me in any way he could. He thought his intimidation tactics would break me—That they would send me running back to him, but they didn't work. I was done being his prisoner.

The day I left, I went to the courthouse and filed a restraining order against Mario. Deep down inside, I knew Veronica worried that I might go back to him—
But I loved my freedom too much to ever return. I had fought too hard and endured too much. I wasn't about to go back to hell.

But Mario wasn't finished with me. He did everything in his power to keep me tied to him. He harassed me on Facebook. When I blocked his number, he used social media to send threats and messages. He created fake posts, fake pages, and fake messages—pretending to be me. He tried hacking into my Facebook account. He even filed a false civil lawsuit against me. He claimed that I had stolen the items I took from the apartment—Even though I had bought them with my own money.

Every time the case didn't go in his favor, he came up with another accusation. It was never-ending. I was fed up. Tired of his games.
Tired of his childishness. Tired of giving him the power to disrupt my peace, so, I relented.

I told the judge—
"If he wants the stuff so badly, he can have it. It's just material things. My peace of mind is more important."

Whatever would make him go away, I was willing to give up.

I arranged for someone to take the items back to the apartment. I just wanted this to be over.

When the guys dropped off the stuff, they told me later that Mario just stood there… staring at me.

He didn't say a word. He just watched. Of course, I never saw him—
I had no idea he was there, but they saw him. And the way they described it chilled me, but I refused to care because it was over.

At last, I could put all of this behind me and finally move on to healing. This chapter of my life was done. And the best chapter of all—
The one where I reclaim my happiness, my peace, and my future—Was just beginning.

CHAPTER 18

While staying with Veronica and her husband, my healing journey finally began. For the first time, I sought out a therapist to help me work through everything I had endured. At first, I wasn't sure if therapy was for me. Could I really open up? Could I trust a complete stranger with my deepest thoughts, feelings, and trauma?

Yes, I had brief therapy after my suicide attempt, but that was only for three days—and I never disclosed the truth about what was really going on. This would be different. This time, I would have to face my pain—not just bury it. I had to take a chance to find out if I was strong enough to do the work, so I committed to it.

I attended therapy twice a week with a therapist that I grew to love. She helped me to really discover who I was, and what my purpose on this earth was. I learned that I was stronger than I gave myself credit for. She allowed me to finally stop blaming myself for what others had done to me. The psychological damage that had been done to me had me trying to justify the behaviors of my abusers.

I rediscovered my faith and joined a church. I received spiritual counseling from my pastor. The sessions reinvigorated my faith in God. It helped me to see that all I went through was not in vain. There truly was a purpose for my pain. My tears of sorrow would be replaced with tears of joy and happiness.

And then, something unexpected happened.

One evening, during Bible study, my pastor asked the group:

"What do you want to discuss today?"

He had no set topic—it was a free discussion day. We could talk about whatever we wanted to talk about within the bible. I'm not sure what came over me, but before I even had time to think, I spoke up.

"How do you forgive?"

The room fell silent. Even my pastor's sharp intake of breath displayed his surprise. And honestly, so was I. I had no idea where the desire to forgive came from, but it had been weighing on me heavily.

The pastor flipped through his Bible and began quoting scriptures about forgiveness. He explained that forgiveness wasn't about excusing the actions of others. It was about freeing yourself from the pain they left behind. As he spoke, something shifted inside me. A sense of peace surrounded me. A weight I didn't even know I was carrying began to lift off my shoulders. And at that moment, I made a decision. I mentally said the names of my abusers. One by one, I said,

"I forgive you."

With each name, I felt myself getting lighter. I forgave my mother. I forgave my father. I forgave Mario. Not because they deserved it—Not because they earned it, but because I deserved peace. I didn't do it for them. I did it for me.

I refused to let hatred and anger weigh me down any longer. I would never forget what they had done to me, but I would no longer carry the burden of unforgiveness. They had all moved on with their lives as if I meant nothing, so why should I waste my life away wondering why they did what they did?

For the first time, I stopped questioning God's intentions for allowing what happened to me. Instead, I embraced the journey ahead. It would no longer be about pain.

It was about healing—mind, body, and soul. The moment I began focusing on healing, new opportunities, and doors started opening for me. The lonely unloved girl who had once moved to a city with nothing and
one was finally blossoming into the concrete rose she was meant to be.

I had a church home.
I had friends who became more like family.
And now? I was a homeowner.
At twenty-five years old, despite everything I had endured, I had saved enough money to put down a down payment on my very first home. And not just any home—A new construction home.

I was building it from the ground up. I was involved in the process from start to finish.
The best part? It was all mine. No one could claim credit for what I had worked so hard for. Against all odds, life was looking up for me.
Veronica and I were neighbors. Our houses were just five doors away from each other. That made it super special to me. I was so happy that because of their help, I was able to break free from the chains that were holding me prisoner. My gratitude for Veronica and her husband stepping in when I was at my darkest hour couldn't be explained in words.

It was almost unbelievable—How ironic that I had once been homeless for six months,
And now, in just six months, I became a homeowner.
For so long, I had been fighting to survive, but now? I was finally living. This was the beginning of something beautiful. This was the life I was meant to have.

The goodness in my life didn't stop there. Despite everything I had been through—every trauma, every setback, every storm—I was able to finally accomplish something that had always felt just out of reach: **I earned my high school diploma.**

During the day, I worked my full-time job, and at night, I **studied online**—dedicating myself to completing something I thought I never would be able to do. I enrolled in **Penn Foster High School** and committed to doing the work, not just for a piece of paper, but for *me*.

At **twenty-five years old**, I did what so many had told me wasn't possible. **I graduated.**

No, it wasn't traditional. There was no cap and gown. No stage. No crowd of cheering classmates or family members. Because the school was based in a different state and I didn't have the financial means to travel, I wasn't able to attend a graduation ceremony, but the day I received my **diploma in the mail**, it was every bit as meaningful.

I had finished high school. I had done it **on my own, and I was proud.**

It was a moment of triumph over everything I had endured. And now? **Next stop: college.** The girl who had once been told she would never amount to anything... The girl who once lived in fear... was now a woman **claiming her education, her future, and her freedom.**

And this time, no one was going to take it away from me again. I had earned my freedom. I fought a good fight and won! I am victorious! I no longer hang my head low in shame because of what was done to me. I am no one's victim! I stand with my head held high. Proud of my resilience and my ability to bend but not break.

CHAPTER 19

Looking back, I can hardly recognize the girl I used to be. The girl who lived in fear, pain, and uncertainty. The girl who spent years being controlled, beaten, and broken. The girl who thought she would never be free.

That girl is gone. In her place stands a woman who fought for her life. A woman who found her voice. A woman who found her strength. A woman who took back everything that was stolen from her—
Her mind. Her body. Her soul.

For so long, I believed I was unworthy of love, happiness, and peace, but now, I know the truth. I am worthy. I am enough. I am unstoppable.

The road to healing wasn't easy by a long shot. It took time, faith, and self-discovery to piece myself back together. I had to learn that forgiveness wasn't for my abusers—it was for me.
I had to accept that what happened to me didn't define me. I had to understand that pain was part of my past—but it wouldn't be part of my future. Now, I stand as a survivor, not a victim.

I have built a life of my own. I have faith, healing, and peace in my life. Everything I went through, every tear I cried, every battle I fought—It led me here.

To a place where I am free. To a place where I am whole. To a place where I am finally free to be me.

If you are reading this, and you feel lost, trapped, or broken, I want you to know one thing:

You are not alone.

I was once where you are—Thinking there was no way out. Believing the pain would never stop. Feeling like I had no options, but I found my way out, and you can, too.

You deserve freedom. You deserve happiness. You deserve to live. If I could survive, rebuild, and thrive, so can you.

My story doesn't end here. This is just the beginning. The next chapter of my life is waiting to be written. And for the first time, I am holding the pen.

I choose happiness. I choose peace. I choose me. The girl who once thought she was powerless has become unstoppable, and this time, I am never looking back.

Acknowledgments

First and foremost, I want to thank **God** for giving me the strength to endure, survive, and rise above the darkness that once tried to consume me. Without His grace and guidance, I wouldn't be here to share my story.

To **Veronica and her husband**, thank you for being my **safe haven**, my protectors, and my family when I had no one else. Your kindness, love, and unwavering support gave me the courage to take the first steps toward freedom.

To my **therapist and spiritual mentors**, thank you for helping me untangle the pain of my past and showing me that healing is not only possible but necessary. Your guidance gave me the tools to rebuild my life and reclaim my power.

To my **friends who became family**, thank you for believing in me, encouraging me, and standing by my side as I learned to live beyond my trauma. Your presence in my life is a gift that I cherish every day.

To every **survivor** reading this book—this is for you.

Your **pain does not define you**. Your **past does not own you**.

You are strong. You are worthy. You are **more than what happened to you**.

Finally, to **myself**—thank you for never giving up.

For every moment you wanted to quit but kept going. For every tear, you cried but still chose to fight. For every time you doubted yourself but pushed forward anyway.

> This journey was never easy, but you made it through.
> And for that, **I am forever proud of you.**

With love and gratitude,

Blaque Diamond

RESOURCES FOR SURVIVORS OF DOMESTIC VIOLENCE, CHILD ABUSE, SEXUAL ABUSE, AND SUICIDE PREVENTION

Emergency Assistance
- Emergency Services (U.S.) – Call 911 if you or someone you know is in immediate danger.

Domestic Violence Support
- National Domestic Violence Hotline
- Phone: 1-800-799-SAFE (7233)
- TTY: 1-800-787-3224
- Website: www.thehotline.org
- Live chat available 24/7.

Love Is Respect (Support for Young Adults and Teens in Abusive Relationships)
- Phone: 1-866-331-9474
- Text: LOVEIS to 22522
- Website: www.loveisrespect.org

Child Abuse Support
- Child help National Child Abuse Hotline
- Phone: 1-800-4-A-CHILD (1-800-422-4453)
- Website: www.childhelp.org
- 24/7 confidential support for children and concerned adults.

Prevent Child Abuse America
- Website: www.preventchildabuse.org

Darkness to Light (Resources on Child Sexual Abuse Prevention & Support)
  o Website: www.d2l.org
  o Helpline: 1-866-FOR-LIGHT (1-866-367-5444)

Sexual Abuse and Assault Support
  o RAINN (Rape, Abuse & Incest National Network)
  o Phone: 1-800-656-HOPE (4673)
  o Website: www.rainn.org
  o Offers 24/7 live chat and local resources.

NSVRC (National Sexual Violence Resource Center)
  o Website: www.nsvrc.org
  o Provides survivor support, education, and referrals.

Suicide Prevention and Crisis Support
  o 988 Suicide & Crisis Lifeline (formerly National Suicide Prevention Lifeline)
  o Phone: 988 (call or text)
  o Website: www.988lifeline.org
  o 24/7 free and confidential support.

Crisis Text Line (Mental Health & Emotional Support)
  o Text: HOME to 741741
  o Website: www.crisistextline.org
  o Available for anyone in distress, offering immediate support.

The Trevor Project (LGBTQ+ Suicide Prevention & Crisis Support)
  o Phone: 1-866-488-7386
  o Text: START to 67867

- Website: www.thetrevorproject.org
- 24/7 crisis support for LGBTQ+ youth.

SAMHSA National Helpline (Mental Health & Substance Use Support)
- Phone: 1-800-662-HELP (4357)
- Website: www.samhsa.gov

Mental Health & Trauma Support
- National Alliance on Mental Illness (NAMI) Helpline
- Phone: 1-800-950-NAMI (6264)
- Text: HELPLINE to 62640
- Website: www.nami.org

RAINN (Rape, Abuse & Incest National Network)
- Phone: 1-800-656-HOPE (4673)
- Website: www.rainn.org

Legal and Advocacy Support
- National Center for Victims of Crime
- Phone: 1-855-4-VICTIM (1-855-484-2846)
- Website: www.victimsofcrime.org

WomensLaw.org (Legal Support for Domestic Violence Survivors)
- Website: www.womenslaw.org

The Joyful Heart Foundation (Healing & Advocacy for Survivors of Abuse and Trauma)
- Website: www.joyfulheartfoundation.org

Support for Male Survivors
- 1in6 (Support for Male Survivors of Sexual Abuse)
- Website: www.1in6.org
- Male Survivor
- Website: www.malesurvivor.org

LGBTQ+ Survivor Resources
- The Anti-Violence Project (LGBTQ+ Domestic & Sexual Violence Support)
- Phone: 1-212-714-1141
- Website: www.avp.org

FORGE (Support for Trans & Nonbinary Survivors of Violence)
- Website: www.forge-forward.org

Human Trafficking Support
- National Human Trafficking Hotline
- Phone: 1-888-373-7888
- Text: HELP or INFO to 233733
- Website: humantraffickinghotline.org

These resources are here to provide help, healing and hope for survivors of abuse, violence, and trauma. You are not alone. Support is available anytime you need it.

About the Author

Blaque Diamond is a totally blind award-winning multi-genre author, poet, motivational speaker, songwriter, and entrepreneur residing in Greensboro, North Carolina. Her writing journey began when she was just eleven years old. She was encouraged to pursue writing by her fifth-grade teacher who saw a natural talent for storytelling in the youngster. Blaque Diamond took her teacher's advice and continued writing into adulthood.

She published her first novel in 2017, and she has published many more titles. She has published 13 books to date on her own, and she has also co-authored 4 additional books with other talented authors. Her published works include short stories, poetry, novellas, and full-length novels. Blaque Diamond writes in many genres including children's literature, poetry, non-fiction, contemporary fiction, and romance.

When she isn't working on her next publication, Blaque Diamond enjoys cooking, traveling, reading, being crafty, writing new music, plotting out her next book, and spending quality time with her significant other and their three children.

Other Books by Blaque Diamond

Love, Lies and Heartbreak Volume 1
His or Her Betrayal?
What You Won't Do
Lyrics of Love
Heart of my words
Dream Paramore
It's Our Anniversary

30-DAY SURVIVOR JOURNAL

These affirmations and journal prompts are designed to encourage self-reflection, empowerment, and healing while helping you reclaim your story and recognize your strength. You are strong, worthy, and capable of creating a beautiful future.

DAY 1

I am not defined by my past; I am empowered by my resilience.

What does strength mean to you, and how have you demonstrated it in your life?

DAY 2

I am unstoppable—I have survived, and I will thrive.

List five things you love about yourself today.

_____

_____

_____

_____

_____

_____

_____

_____

_____

_____

_____

_____

_____

DAY 3

My journey is valid, and my healing is important.

*What are three ways I have grown
since my healing journey began?*

DAY 4

I am proud of how far I have come.

Describe a safe place—real or imagined—where you feel completely at peace.

DAY 5

I trust myself and my ability to create a beautiful life.

What is one small act of self-care you can do for yourself today?

DAY 6

My survival is a testament to my power.

Write a letter to your past self, offering kindness and encouragement.

DAY 7

My voice matters, and I have the right to speak my truth.

What makes you feel empowered, and how can you invite more of that into your life?

DAY 8

My body is mine, and I honor it with love and care.

What are three positive affirmations you can repeat to yourself when you feel down?

DAY 9

I release the pain of my past and embrace the joy of my future.

Describe a time when you overcame something difficult. How did you do it?

DAY 10

I am rebuilding my life with love and purpose.

What is something you are proud of yourself for today?

_____
_____
_____
_____
_____
_____
_____
_____
_____
_____
_____
_____

DAY 11

I attract peace, love, and safety into my life.

How can you show yourself the same love and compassion you would give a close friend?

DAY 12

I am worthy of love, respect, and kindness.

What are five things you are grateful for in your life right now?

DAY 13

I choose to love myself unconditionally.

Write about a person (real or fictional) who inspires you and why.

DAY 14

I am healing at my own pace, and that is okay.

What are some healthy boundaries you have set or want to set for yourself?

DAY 15

I am not responsible for the harm done to me,
but I am responsible for my healing.

If you could give yourself one piece of advice, what would it be?

DAY 16

Healing is my birthright, and I claim it with courage.

Describe a moment in your life when you felt truly free.

DAY 17

I am whole, even as I continue to heal.

What dreams or goals do you have for your future?

DAY 18

My trauma does not define me—my strength does.

*What is something that brings you peace,
and how can you incorporate more of it into your life?*

DAY 19

I deserve to experience joy, love, and happiness.

Write a letter to someone who hurt you—without sending it— expressing your feelings and reclaiming your power.

DAY 20

I am strong, and I have survived what was meant to break me.

What are three positive words that describe you today?

DAY 21

I am allowed to set boundaries and protect my peace.

Describe what self-love means to you and how you can practice it daily.

DAY 22

Each day, I grow stronger, wiser, and more at peace.

What fears or doubts are you ready to let go of?

DAY 23

I forgive myself for anything I once blamed myself for.

*Write about a time when you felt happy and safe.
What made it special?*

DAY 24

I am enough just as I am.

What are three things you can do to nurture your mind, body, and soul?

DAY 25

No one has the power to silence me—I own my story.

List five ways you have taken control of your healing journey.

DAY 26

I deserve to be safe, happy, and free.

Write a love letter to your future self, reminding yourself of your worth and strength.

_____

_____

_____

_____

_____

_____

_____

_____

_____

_____

_____

_____

DAY 27

My past does not dictate my future; I create my own destiny.

What are three positive habits you can develop to support your healing?

DAY 28

I release shame and embrace my worth.

Describe what a perfect day of peace and joy would look like for you.

DAY 29

I am courageous, and I rise above my past.

What qualities make you a survivor, and how do you embody them every day?

DAY 30

Every step I take toward healing is a victory.

End the month by writing about the progress you've made and celebrating your resilience.

www.ingramcontent.com/pod-product-compliance
Lightning Source LLC
Chambersburg PA
CBHW061749070526
44585CB00025B/2839